PUT GOD FIRST

By
BURKE CULPEPPER

First Fruits Press
Wilmore, Kentucky
c2016

Put God First. By Burke Culpepper.

First Fruits Press, ©2016

Previously published by the Pentecostal Publishing Company, ©1925

ISBN: 9781621715207 (print) 9781621715214 (digital) 9781621715221 (kindle)

Digital version at http://place.asburyseminary.edu/firstfruitsheritagematerial/124/

First Fruits Press is a digital imprint of the Asbury Theological Seminary, B.L. Fisher Library. Asbury Theological Seminary is the legal owner of the material previously published by the Pentecostal Publishing Co. and reserves the right to release new editions of this material as well as new material produced by Asbury Theological Seminary. Its publications are available for noncommercial and educational uses, such as research, teaching and private study. First Fruits Press has licensed the digital version of this work under the Creative Commons Attribution Noncommercial 3.0 United States License. To view a copy of this license, visit http://creativecommons.org/licenses/by-nc/3.0/us/.

For all other uses, contact:

First Fruits Press
B.L. Fisher Library
Asbury Theological Seminary
204 N. Lexington Ave.
Wilmore, KY 40390
http://place.asburyseminary.edu/firstfruits

Culpepper, Burke.

   Put god first / by Burke Culpepper.
   Wilmore, Kentucky : First Fruits Press, ©2016.
   168 pages ; 21 cm.
   "A series of evangelistic sermons delivered through the South and West."
   Reprint. Previously published: Louisville, Kentucky : Pentecostal Publishing Company, ©1925.
   ISBN: 9781621715207 (pbk.)

   1. Evangelistic sermons. 2. Sermons, American. I. Title.

BV3797 .C85 2016

Cover design by Jonathan Ramsay

asburyseminary.edu
800.2ASBURY
204 North Lexington Avenue
Wilmore, Kentucky 40390

First Fruits Press
The Academic Open Press of Asbury Theological Seminary
204 N. Lexington Ave., Wilmore, KY 40390
859-858-2236
first.fruits@asburyseminary.edu
asbury.to/firstfruits

PUT GOD FIRST

By

Rev. BURKE CULPEPPER, D. D.

A series of evangelistic sermons
delivered through the south and west

PENTECOSTAL PUBLISHING COMPANY
LOUISVILLE, KENTUCKY.

COPYRIGHTED, 1925,
BY
PENTECOSTAL PUBLISHING COMPANY
LOUISVILLE, KY

A Father's Introduction
By
Rev. John B. Culpepper, D.D.

By these presents, I wish to introduce to you Burke Culpepper, whose sermons lie before you, and in the perusal of which you will find both pleasure and profit.

In the forty-five years of his life, he has spent fully thirty of it, before the public, as singer, children's preacher, my revival associate; and for fifteen years, has held so many great meetings throughout the South, and been so widely reported, that his name is a household word, rather than a young author needing an introduction.

I sustain a rare relation to the Methodist church, and the general public, being a minister, with two other sons who are preachers, in now calling attention to a volume the contents of which, when spoken, has warmed the hearts of thousands, alarmed the guilty fears of thousands, impelled many thousands of convicted men and women to seek shelter under the soul canopying cross of Christ, while gladdening the hearts of the great leaders of our Zion, as they saw her numbers increasing under his garnering hand. In perusing my son's manuscript, I have noted, with joy, that he has presented only Christ's view of God and our destiny—the only one in any religion or philosophy, not degrading to the worshipper.

To be a great preacher, one must take Christ's view of the soul, whose greatest loss is to God, its maker, Jesus its redeemer, the Holy Spirit, its regenerator, and then to the soul itself.

A great sermon or speech or book, must have great thoughts, or emotions, clothed in becoming language.

God, in matter, expresses Himself, in wisdom and force, while His revelation to our souls requires our reason, conscience, will, in which realm alone can personality be found. In this latter field the preacher lives and operates. We are familiar with ambassadors, negotiating between states, great business, social, civil, military and peace-footing affairs; but the preacher is heaven's diplomat from heaven to earth, and from earth back to heaven, and he holds a life tenure.

There is not a dull or an idle hour in his life, from the moment of his appointment, until he is recalled, or complete reconciliation is effected between these two great countries, in both of which he holds citizenship.

Science says that nature has created nothing new, for inconceivable ages, and yet we all love to see, hear, tell of something new. It is in this realm of making men new, and building a new heaven and earth, that we best know God, and this is the preacher's ever-thrilling work, making souls new.

No wonder that John Elliot stopped making money, forsook the haunts of civilization, bereaved

A FATHER'S INTRODUCTION

himself of comfort and culture, and lived among Indians, to help Jesus develop His sermon to Nicodemus.

It was not so hard to forecast the life of the author of this book, for immediately, upon his arrival in our Georgia home, he started out with an echo-waking whistle, full head of steam, throttle wide open, little use for brakes, and has never been on a siding, because he was on another man's time, and thus far, has never rung down late at the depot, nor gone for repairs.

If Burke Culpepper has one particle of envy, or pulpit jealousy, I never saw it, and when with me, his soul seemed to be full if I was treated right, and if the meeting was a go—wherever he was in the conflict.

When I paid him twenty-five dollars a meeting, then fifty, then one third, then half, he invariably asked if I could spare that much, and if I thought he was worth it to me, and if I was satisfied with what he had done.

I hear that question, sometimes in my dreams, for when he went out for himself, I turned down his chair.

The true minister is a philanthropist, going about doing good by teaching people to elevate all lower, or common and often useless things, into gardens, homes vineyards and flowered yards, with houses frescoed, pictured, filled with laughter and song, as dollars are translated into terms of sentiment and service. The pulpiteer and pastor holds the balance of power, in teaching the lowly to laugh, the poor to pray, the sick to smile, the sinking to shout, and the languishing that they will live. There is no field for oratory like the preacher's field, and no orator like the man who knows his Christ is above him, interceding while he administers the grace of recovery, in proportion to God's purpose, and his commissioned ability to proclaim the year of Jubilee. With a sunrise of joy in his own soul, and a scorching pity for the lost and despairing, he goes everywhere, playing upon every key in human hearts, intellects and will, returning laden with sheaves of liberty to the captives, water to the famishing, mountains of myrrh to the sick, and a home to each wanderer.

We are proud of our educational system, and we set it before the world with much boasting; but the preacher has the first and last word in real learning, for he teaches us to know God, and Jesus Christ whom He has sent, and he tells us simply and plainly, of all the relations we sustain to each other, to this world and the next. From him we learn that God is love, and that love established law; that the things which God forbids, would have hurt us anyhow, and that which He enjoins would have been for our happiness and good, any how—all of which is proof, incontestable, that God is love.

No torrential mountain stream can leap and laugh, dive and defy, spray and spring, sing and shout, like unto the eloquent lips, feet, hands, eyes of a preacher on fire from within and without

A FATHER'S INTRODUCTION

aflame from reading his commission to the lost, while he shouts down into their pit, that they can climb out and live. From a central deep, yet never found, the tides return and defy all resistance rolling in, rolling on, rolling over, rolling ever—here billowing, yonder spraying, and yonder garnishing in whitecap—never failing to awaken admiration, and awe, and to me this is but a faint type of the force and onrush of a man called of God to save lost souls.

And like old ocean, he can play every human cord, from a thunderous command to surrender, to the sobbing to sleep on mother's soft bosom, while the mother heart rythms her lullabies to her babe—so the preacher brings the tired, weary soul to Jesus, and again mounts the pulpit.

I have heard the lawyer appeal from his opponent's declaration, to former decisions; from the rulings of the bench; from the verdict of the jury, and I have been excited with their excitement; but when the preacher holds up the book of God, men know that the highest reason for attention, and obedience has been offered, and that it is as if Jesus Christ had the floor.

Jesus was the great doctor, and he sent out the preacher, with remedies for the body, mind and soul, and commanded them to heal the sick, and until now, the preacher holds the chest containing the most effective cure for mind and heart. Send for him; let him tear from his great prescription book, the very thing you need.

A FATHER'S INTRODUCTION

The preacher and his messages are like a stream in the south—rising in the fastnesses of man's dire need, and God's undiscouragable purpose, trickling over ledge and lea, asking a missionary contribution from every dewdrop, every silvery mist, every gentle shower—thus ever increasing in volume, until it bears on its broad bosom, the commerce of church and civilization a veritable Mississippi at the gates of New Orleans, or a mighty ocean rivaling Amazon.

Nothing will ever take the preacher's place, until the lines between ear, heart, mind, soul, destiny are all down, which will proclaim the last grain out of the urn of time, and the last resource of Christ has been expended for men's souls. You can't get rid of the preacher, except by heeding him. He is like the poor—with you always. Jonah was a Jew and a preacher, and they are both indigestible, by any alchemy, chyle or chyme, known to sinners. The preacher should be first at the baptismal font, and it is he, who will stand above you and say ashes to ashes—dust to dust.

Then you don't wonder that I esteem it an honor of high class, to recommend this young man of God, and to endorse and commend this book of appeals to men to be reconciled to God.

A Mother's Indorsement
By
Mrs. Melvina Culpepper.

I wish to say that, before Burke was many hours old, the Master of Men told me that He had entrusted to me the rearing of another preacher, as He had in the case of his older brother.

I could never dream, or draw, or write poetry; but whether my baby cooed, or cried; whether he was frolicsome or sick; whether I rocked him to sleep or kissed him off to school, I always saw him in the pulpit. I have ever considered myself the happiest of Georgia girls, in having a husband and three splendid boys to preach.

I will be glad for you to find pleasure in the sermons of Burke—just Burke, my darling boy—while thinking of a mother's investment, a mother's gratitude, a mother's love.

*Lovingly
dedicated to my wife,
Kate.*

TABLE OF CONTENTS.

Chapter.		Page.
I.	Put God First	15
II.	Jotham's Parable	32
III.	The Incarnation	44
IV.	Immortality	62
V.	The Holy Spirit	73
VI.	Samson	84
VII.	The Prodigal Son	107
VIII.	The Great Salvation	119
IX.	Winding The Reel	140

CHAPTER 1.
PUT GOD FIRST

But God said unto him, thou fool, this night thy soul shall be required of thee: then whose shall those things be, which thou hast provided?" (Luke 12:20).

The sin of covetousness is one of the deadliest sins that attack the soul of man. Jesus' ringing rebuke to that brother who wanted him to referee a family estate shows His attitude toward worldly possessions.

When the rich young ruler came running to Jesus, kneeling at his feet, calling him "good Master" and inquiring the way of life, Jesus touched his only vulnerable point, covetousness. Grieved, he turned away and went back to his money-counting, and will be known through the ages as the young man of the great refusal.

Dives went to hell not because he was rich, but because he worshipped riches. He didn't possess his money; his money possessed him. Abraham was rich, but God came first with him. You see this in his agreement with Lot.

Judas Iscariot carried the bag, and its contents were more precious to him than the words that fell from the Master's lips. The alabaster box of spikenard, while delightsome and fragrant to those who loved Jesus, was offensive to Judas, who wanted to put its value in his bag; and finally he became so eaten up with avarice that he sold his Lord for thirty pieces of silver and delivered Him with a kiss.

This ancient barn builder of our text had no true appreciation of relative values. A leading attorney of Memphis, Tennessee, lost his beautiful house and furnishings by fire. A friend said to him, "I see from the morning paper that your home burned last night." "Oh no," replied the attorney, "you are mistaken; my home didn't burn. All the fires of earth could not destroy my home. It was my house that burned!" Quite a difference.

> The walls of a house may be builded of wood.
> Its foundations of brick or of stone;
> But a genuine home is an exquisite thing.
> For it's builded of heart-throbs alone.
>
> The price of a house may be reckoned at once,
> And paid with a handful of gold;
> But the price of a home very few can compute,
> And that price they have never yet told.
>
> The rooms of a house may be stately and grand,
> Their adornment a triumph of art;
> But beauty of home is the final result
> Of the toil of an unselfish heart.
>
> A house may be burned, may be sold or exchanged,
> Nor the loss of one's peace interfere;
> But the loss of a home—how it crushes the heart!
> For our homes we all love and revere.
>
> Of houses a man may possess many scores
> Yet his poverty lead to despair;
> But an honorable man, in a home of his own,
> Must be counted a true millionaire.*

*J H Sykes

Aaron Burr, when a student at Princeton University, said to an earnest friend who was begging him to consider the claims of the Master, "If Jesus Christ will let me alone I will never bother Him." You know the result. This gifted man, once the vice-president of the United States, became a traitor to his country and flag, stained his hands with another man's blood and died on foreign soil, Christless.

The greatest sin of the present age is secularity. God is not first, but last and, with many, as with the barn-builder, He is left out altogether.

HE LEFT GOD OUT OF HIS PLANS

"And he thought within himself, saying, what shall I do; because I have nowhere to bestow my fruits? And he said, this will I do, I will pull down my barns and build greater, and there will I bestow all my fruits and my goods." He left God out of his plans. God had given him the sunshine and the rain; had given him health. And yet he does not propose to pay back one cent. No, "I"ll build me bigger barns and there will I put my goods." Poor fool! And yet thousands today have done and are doing the same thing. I care not what vocation you have selected, get God into your plans. If you would be a physician, call in consultation the Great Physician. If you would be a lawyer, let the great Advocate of heaven look over your briefs. If you would be a farmer, let him who sows "the good seed" impregnate your life. Oh, whatever you do, or be, get God into your plans. Put God first.

I once read the story of a bright young man who, through the benefactions of a wealthy old gentleman, was enabled to attend college and graduate, which he did with high honor. He concluded before going to Denver, his chosen field of labor, to visit his benefactor, and tell him of his plans. After reaching the old gentleman's home, and thanking him again and again for his great kindness to him, by placing within his grasp a weapon with which he could successfully fight the battles of life, he said, "Major, I thought it really due you to let you know my plans and get your acquiescence." "Well," said the major, "what do you propose to do?" Said the young man: "I have chosen law, as you know, and am going to Denver to put out my shingle and begin." "And what then?" asked the major. "Well," replied the young man, "I hope to be successful, even from the first. Of course I expect to save my money, buy books, be studious and make a name." "And what then?" again asked the venerable man. "By that time I shall probably marry some sweet girl, build me a home, be happy and enjoy a lucrative practice." "Well, what then?" "Oh, by that time I'll have money enough saved to be comfortable, and my reputation will be such that I will take only such cases as pay well, and as my wife and children ride down the street the people will say, 'Yonder goes the colonel's family.' In other words, I hope to be famous." "Well, what then?" "I guess by that time my children will be grown and

I'll see them through to success as you have me." "Well, what then?" "Oh, I'll be quite old by that time. Guess I will sit in the corner till the death angel comes." Then the old man shouted, "Well, what then, young man?" He had laid his plans one by one, step by step, to the very verge of the grave, where he must meet God, and yet had left God out. Oh, young man, put God first. Get God into your plans, for—hear me—God will get into them somehow. You had better invite Him in. The first monumental blunder the rich fool made was to leave God out of his plans.

HE WAS A MATERIALIST

Man is body and soul. And just as you have to take care of your body, so you must look after your soul and its interests. Your body is finite and perishable; your soul is imperishable, immortal.

<blockquote>To lose your wealth is much, to lose your health is more;
To lose your soul is such a loss as no man can restore."</blockquote>

How men strive to bring plenty and comfort to their body, which will rot in the grave, when their soul, which is to live when the stars are dead, is neglected! This fool thought his soul could subsist on the same things as his body. "Soul, take thine own ease, eat, drink and be merry, thou hast much goods laid up for many years."

How could his soul take its ease? There is but one thing which can satisfy a human soul, and that is Jesus. Just as the light is adapted to the eye, sound to the ear drum, so is your soul adapted to

God and God to it. Money cannot satisfy the soul. Beautiful, palatial brown-stone houses on be-flowered boulevards, will not bring peace and contentment in the dying hour. "God is a spirit, and they that worship Him, must worship him in spirit and in truth." A friend gives me a beautiful little bird which I take home in a cheap wooden cage. I hang the cage on the wall in my room, but the little bird will not sing. I change him from one part of the room to another. Still he droops and pines. It bothers me, and I say, "What's the matter, little bird? Why don't you sing?" Oh, I know what's the matter. He can't be happy in that cheap cage. I'll buy him a golden cage, with silver cups from which to eat, and crystal basin in which to bathe his downy feathers. How magnificent you look, little bird, in your golden prison! But still he droops. I take him out to the flower garden where the sun is shining and the air is balmy. Still he looks sick. Maybe he cannot sing. I gently reach my hand into the cage, take the little fellow out and, stroking his bright plumage say, as I open his tiny mouth, "Can't you sing, my bird?" Just then he leaps from my hand to the limb of a tree. I try in vain to catch him. See him as he sits there, so saucily looking down at me, preening his ruffled feathers! He gazes at me a moment, then into the air he flips and, with a song which almost bursts his throat, he soars toward the sun, singing back to me. "Farewell, golden cage and silver cups; I have found my home and now I will sing." How can your soul "eat, drink and be merry" when you feed it on material things only? What would you think of a man who, instead of giving his horse corn and oats each morning before driving him, would go out to the stable and read the twenty-third Psalm to him? Or instead of giving bran to his cow before milking her, would throw her a copy of "Old Mother Goose" rhymes? You say such a man is a fool. And that is why God called the man of my text, a fool. He thought his soul could subsist on the things which were only adapted to his body. Many a man tries to feed his soul on corner lots, stiff bank accounts and fertile farms, and then wonders why he is not happy. How can your soul be happy on such diet? Look at that herd of foolish women who feed their souls on silks and satins, on ostrich plumes and bridge parties. "Eat, drink and be merry," they say to their souls, while their souls faintly call back, "We want the bread of life." There are many kinds of fools in the world. There are intellectual fools, society fools, gambling fools, drinking fools and many other kinds of fools too numerous to mention. Some one has said, "Everybody is some kind of fool." But the biggest of all fools is the money fool.

This man was a money fool. Very few people have sense enough to have money. Did you ever see a man who suddenly came into possession of a fortune? Now watch him! The chances are he will just about quit going to church, and will drop family prayer altogether. He is so important and so conceited it is disgusting to be around him. And listen to him, as he puts his hands in his pockets and talks learnedly about things great and small. See his ignorant wife and green children bloom into society. Money turned them fools. Take their money away and they will come to themselves. My father was pastor of a man down in Georgia who was quite wealthy, but irreligious. My father had tried in vain to be a blessing to him, but you could see he was suspicious of him, thinking he was after his money. One day the man was taken sick. He grew rapidly worse from the first. It was a pitiable sight to see the poor sinner lying there, talking about his money, which was in a large chest near him. Oh, how he hated to leave it! He became suspicious of his wife and children, and forbade them in his room. The day he died he requested the doctor to take a key from off his wrist and unlock the chest and pile the money on the bed beside him. He then said, "Doctor, hand me my gun." The physician, knowing he could not use it, handed it to him, or rather laid it across his lap. Then said the poor fool, "Now, doctor, you get out of here." When the man of medicine returned, but a few minutes later, he was dead. He had his money, didn't he? No! His money had him! Oh, these money fools, who think not of their souls, but of their money. Money is a useful thing in its place, and you can so use it while you live, that instead of being a black vulture, probing your conscience in the dying hour, the eagles on the dollars you have made will turn to singing nightingales, and make your death bed "as soft as downy pillows are." Joaquin Miller beautifully and truthfully sings:

> Carve your name high o'er the drifting sand,
> Where the steadfast rocks defy decay;
> All you can hold in your cold, dead hand
> Is what you have given away.
>
> Count your wide conquests o'er sea and land,
> Heap up your gold, and hoard as you may;
> All you can hold in your cold, dead hand
> Is what you have given away.
>
> Build your pyramids, skyward, let them rise,
> Stand gazed at by millions, cultured they say;
> All you can hold in your cold, dead hand,
> Is what you have given away.
>
> Silver and gold and jewels so grand,
> King of the saloon, or mart for a day;
> Yet all you can hold in your cold, dead hand
> Is what you have given away.

Mr. Cole told me that when he was pastor in Chicago many years ago this very sad incident occurred. While out visiting one afternoon he called on one of his most prominent families. Just as he was about to leave one of the young ladies said, "Oh, Mr. Cole, let me show you something exquisite," and one of the girls ran hurriedly upstairs and returned. She and her sister each held a tailor's box in hand, which bore the stamp of some Paris dress-maker. Georgia said, "Isn't this the prettiest thing you ever saw?" (taking a beautiful dress from the box and holding it in front of Mr. Cole.) "The trimmings alone on each of these dresses cost papa fifteen hundred dollars; he brought them from Paris last week. We are going to wear them to the Christmas ball." Mr. Cole said,

"Girls, which do you think would please God more: for you to wear them to the ball, or give them to your pastor and let him advertise them in the papers, sell them and give the money to the mission fields?" "Not on your life," said Georgia. "I'd dance in this gown if I knew it would cost me my soul." The younger sister said nothing, but turned pale and looked at Georgia. "Well, I just thought I would ask the question," said Mr. Cole. "Good evening." The next day the preacher received a note from the younger sister in which she told him his question had startled her, and that she had not slept a wink that night, and further she had decided he might take her dress and sell it and turn the money into the mission treasury. Georgia went to the ball and had a good time. The papers complimented her lovely Paris gown. While dancing, however, becoming very warm, she ran to the window and caught cold, which settled in her lungs and terminated in pneumonia, from which death resulted in eight days. The day she died she asked that Mr. Cole be called in. When he got there she was nearly gone, but seeing him, she requested that the ball dress be brought to her. Raising a white, bejeweled hand, she pointed to the dress and said, "Oh, beautiful Paris gown, I gave my soul for thee!" Oh, men and women, I beg you not to place anything ahead of your soul and its welfare. *Put God first.*

Life is real, life is earnest,
And the grave is not its goal;
Dust thou art, to dust returneth,
Was not spoken of the soul.

HE THOUGHT HIS GOODS WERE HIS OWN

"And he thought within himself, saying, what shall I do, because I have no room where to bestow my fruits." There were churches to be built, ministers to be educated, heathen to be saved, bibles to be scattered, widows and orphans to be fed, none of which he thought of.

He failed to recognize the blessed law of stewardship. In a sense a man's possessions do belong to him, but in a higher sense they do not. A man may belong to himself, but let his wife and children get sick, he must give up business, pleasure and everything that he may go to their assistance. He is subject to their call. A man may belong to himself, but let his country go to war, he is subject to its call. Now, in this sense, a man's possessions may be his own, but he must remember that God, who has prospered him and blessed him with sunshine and showers, with health and other facilities for the acquisition of these earthly goods, has a right, a higher right, a just right, to call on him whenever He may see fit. *Put God first.* One of the finest signs of our times is the disposition of rich men to regard their vast wealth as an opportunity to bless the world.

Yes, whatever we have is God's first, then ours. Mothers, if God calls upon you to give up your darling little babe, remember it belongs to Him. If He sees fit to take your health, remember he has a right, and knows best. And should He take your property, remember He loves you and is doing it for your ultimate good. Oh, don't rebel against the will of God.

HE THOUGHT HE HAD A LEASE ON LIFE

"Soul, thou hast much goods laid up for many years." Of all the stupendous blunders of this reckless man, this was the most monumental. And it is the great blunder men are making today, as no man has any assurance of life.

> Death rides on every passing breeze,
> And lurks in every flower.

No man knows who will be the next to die. I care not how robust and hearty, how fair and young you may be, just listen and you will hear death muttering:

> I have marked you for my own,
> I will claim you bye and bye.

There are as many short graves as long ones. Death is no respecter of persons. He comes to the mansion as well as to the hovel.

When I was in Mississippi, several years ago, holding a meeting, the organist said: "You will have to excuse me this afternoon, Brother Culpepper; I can't be at church." Said I, "Why? I need you very much." She replied, "One of my friends has just died." I said, "You are excused; you have my sympathy." The next afternoon at three I preached her funeral. How little did she expect to die so soon when she was talking to me.

A lady, who moved in the highest circles of society, one evening became convinced of sin and

PUT GOD FIRST 27

alarmed about her condition. Deep conviction followed. She struggled against it. She thought of her many engagements and her social position in life. Conscience said, "Decide for Christ now." The world whispered, "Not just yet, but by and by; such a step should not be taken hastily." In this state of perplexity and distress she retired to her room. As she did not appear the following morning, and did not answer the call, her room was entered. Oh, what a sight for the family! The stillness of death reigned. There lay the body cold and lifeless. Her diary lay open upon the table. There were two entries made the previous evening: "I am determined this day six months to give up the world and become a Christian." But as if the conflict in her soul had deepened and conscience had cried still louder, she had made a second entry: "This day one month I am determined to be done with the world and follow Christ." "But God said, this night thy soul shall be required of thee." And what became of that soul? And what, oh sinner, would become of your soul if you should die tonight? And perhaps you may. Be warned by this example of the danger of delay, and hasten to get right with God.

He thought he had a lease on life. "Soul, thou hast much goods laid up for many years." If I could convince you that you might die tonight you would seek God. While my father and I were engaged in a meeting in Columbus, Georgia, this incident occurred: One night in the great tent, while hundreds were coming forward for prayer, I noticed a young man about thirty years old, crying. Stepping over to him I said, "Friend, go forward and give your heart to God." But he replied, "Not tonight, sir, not tonight." I insisted, but again he said. "Not tonight: I will go tomorrow night, I declare I will." I passed on. The next afternoon, walking into the tent to preach, I noticed that the people were hurriedly leaving, and upon inquiry I found that the excavation which had been arranged for the water mains had closed in, burying ten men. I hurried down to the scene of horror. When taken out all but two were dead. Imagine, if you can, my surprise when I saw that the last one removed was the young man who had but the evening before said to me, "Not tonight, sir, not tonight." He said "Tomorrow night," but God said "tonight."

GOD'S VERDICT

"Thou fool." Now, that was not the verdict of his wife. Doubtless she considered him faultless. Many a woman will have to give an account for the influence she had over her husband, or could have had. A great many women seem not to care how hard their husbands have to work, or what may become of their souls hereafter, just so they dress them in the latest "agony." There will be many men lost at last, of whom it can be said, "wife-damned." I have no idea but that his children thought him perfect. Who knows but the minister who preached his funeral preached him "straight into glory." Of course the Lord's verdict was not that of the town in which he lived. They considered him anything but a fool. All were glad to be counted among his friends; envied were those fortunate enough to be invited to his mansion. Oh, how true, that "man looketh on the outward appearance, but God looketh on the heart."

Remember, sinner, that "the earth passeth away, and the fashions thereof; but they who do the will of God shall abide forever." Did you ever stop to think of that word "lost?" Have you thought of the awful state of a soul banished from the presence of God? Of one whose only consolation is found in looking through the past and thinking of the transient pleasures he enjoyed in this world, while God through His Holy Spirit, His word and His faithful followers was warning him to forsake his sinful life, seek salvation and flee the wrath to come? But alas! he waited too long. Do not sell your soul for that which will perish with the using.

On one occasion when Rowland Hill was preaching to a vast concourse of people in one of the parks in England, Lady Erskine, who had heard much of him and was anxious to hear and see him, drove out in her carriage to where he was preaching the gospel. Mr. Hill had been preaching some fifteen minutes when she drove up. She opened the door of her carriage and looked at him. The great evangelist paused a moment, closed his bible, and then announced to the audience that he had something to sell. Every one was amazed to think he would stop in the midst of such a wonderful discourse to sell something. What could it be? was the question in every heart. Imagine Lady Erskine's consternation when the man of God, pointing his finger at her, announced the soul of Lady Ann Erskine for sale. "Do I hear a bid? What am I offered for this proud, haughty woman's soul?" Lady Ann Erskine said, "Drive on, coachman," but he had his eyes on the marvelous preacher, and seemed unable to move. "Ah," said Mr. Hill, "yonder is a bidder for your soul. He offers you worldly honors, worldly pleasures, so-called peace, but you must take death and hell, at last. Will you sell for that? Do I hear another bid? Yes, there stands a Being whose face is as fair as the morning, but whose hands have been pierced with cruel nails. He offers you happiness, peace and joy here and a fadeless crown of righteousness beyond the river of death. Now, which will you take, Lady Erskine —the devil, or Jesus with the nail prints in his hands?" With tears dropping from her eyes she leaped from the carriage and, extending a bejeweled hand, said, "Oh, Mr. Hill, I will take the one with the nail-pierced hands."

Sinner, I commend Jesus to you. Accept Him now and be ready when the death angel knocks, or when Jesus shall rend the heavens and come in His glory to judge the world.

AT NIGHT.

When noonday's sun is buried low
Within a casket in the west,
When evening breezes come and go
Like sighings of an anxious breast,
When blackened shadows slowly creep
O'er wooded moor and pathless sod,
Then nature lays her down to sleep
And all are well who trust in God;
Then what of him who, robbed of light,
Trembles and starts with venomed fright,
The wretch who gropes all full of sin,
Tormented by the hell within,
Alone upon the road at night;
Whose life is full of theft and lies,
Who totters, falls and falling dies.
Upon the road of sin at night,
Alone upon the road at night?

Yea, what of him whose sun shall set
Amid the silvery clouds of time,
Who sees the shadows, black as jet,
Come thick and fast from that dread clime,
Peopled with shrouds, the well-fed tomb,
The rotting flesh and broken bone;
Nor hears aught save an endless moan?
Nor hears aught same an endless moan?
Oh, what of him who, robbed of light,
Trembles and starts with venomed fright;
The wretch who gropes, all full of sin,
Tormented by the hell within,
Alone upon the road at night?
Who falls and falling ne'er shall rise.
Who dies and dying never dies.
Upon the road at night,
Alone upon the road at night?*

*Selected.

CHAPTER II.

JOTHAM'S PARABLE

> I think that I shall never see
> A poem lovely as a tree.
>
> A tree whose hungry mouth is prest
> Against the earth's sweet flowing breast;
>
> A tree that looks to God all day,
> And lifts her leafy arms to pray;
>
> A tree that may in summer wear
> A nest of robins in her hair;
>
> Upon whose bosom snow has lain;
> Who intimately lives with rain.
>
> Poems are made by fools like me,
> But only God can make a tree.*

Trees are older than man. See Genesis 1:2. It was from a tree that Eve took the forbidden fruit and started the race away from God. (Genesis 3:6.) The destinies of men and nations have been peculiarly associated with trees. I remember that a peach tree in my mother's back yard had much to do with forming my character. Men go to trees for recreation, for consolation, for help in their problems. Zaccheus climbed up into a sycamore tree to see Jesus. Every Ty Cobb and Babe Ruth, from the country sand lots to the great baseball parks of the metropolitan cities where all America gathers for its national pastime, listens for the

---
*Joyce Kilmer

crack of the white ash against the horse hide. Red cedar for pencils, walnut for gun stocks, hickory for ax handles, automobile spokes and plow stocks; yellow pine for houses and cypress for shingles. Lignum-vitae combines the required density and toughness and natural lubricant for the propeller shaft bearings of steamships. The masters of the violin will tell you it takes spruce for the belly, and pernambuco wood for the bow, if high art is to be obtained. Turkish boxwood is sought for fine engravings. The Arabians put the palm tree to nearly three hundred uses.

The late Senator Tom Watson, of Georgia, wrote beautifully of trees as follows:

"One great soldier is commemorated throughout the world by cuttings of the willow under which he used to rest, as he meditated upon the world that he had lost.

"Another great soldier said with his last breath. 'Let us cross over the river and rest under the shade of the trees.'

"Still another soldier and great man, whose monument towers above all others on earth, spent his last afternoon of out-door life marking the inferior trees, which were to be felled, in order that the grandeur of Mt. Vernon might not be marred.

"Napoleon said that the most beautiful sight to his eyes was a lovely girl, clad in white, walking on the green grass under the trees.

"When Aristotle and Plato taught the sublimest

lessons of antiquity they walked with their students under the trees.

"When Julius Caesar wished to win forever the love of the Roman people he gave them his gardens and his groves on the Tiber.

"When the Babylonian king wished to deeply please his bride, a mountain girl, he built for her the hanging gardens, one of the seven wonders of the world, in which every tree and flower grew.

"The immortal sermon of Krishna was preached under a tree, and these noble words of the lofty-minded mystic are strangely like those of the sermon on the mount.

"There is no music like that of the wind in the trees—the weird dirge of the pines, the wild flutter of the maple, the whisperings of the white birches and the hoarse roar of the oaks.

"Nothing more beautiful can be seen than the red beech bursting into its Easter dress; nothing more regal than the hickory's blaze of yellow-gold in the autumn sun; nothing more gorgeous than the Tyrian purple that the Spanish oak wears—wears proudly when other trees are reefing their sails for winter, and their sere leaves have come sighing to the ground.

"Spring and summer and autumn have power to glorify the trees, and winter is powerless to strip them of their beauty.

"The sleet may come, but it armors them in silver; the snow may come, but its winding sheet does not enshroud the dead; the winds may toss their leafless limbs back and forth, but there are voices in these winds, and we hear our names called in the night—called by voices that we shall not otherwise hear."

Turn to the index of your bible and find the word tree. Look up the many references and ponder the lessons that God teaches us through the trees. You will not only be surprised but greatly benefited.

I think that the parable of Jotham, from his rocky crag pulpit, not only was the utterance of a true prophet but was more beautiful than any words ever spoken concerning trees. In his noble parable he beautifully defends his illustrious father, rebukes the seditious Abimelech, warns the duped people and points a lesson worthy of modern application.

The trees went forth on a time to anoint a king over them; and they said unto the olive tree, Reign thou over us.

But the olive tree said unto them, Should I leave my fatness, wherewith by me they honor God and man, and go to be promoted over the trees?

And the trees said to the fig tree, Come thou, and reign over us.

But the fig tree said unto them, Should I forsake my sweetness, and my good fruit, and go to be promoted over the trees?

Then said the trees unto the vine, Come thou, and reign over us.

And the vine said unto them, Should I leave my vine, which cheereth God and man, and go to be promoted over the trees?

Then said all the trees unto the bramble, Come thou, and reign over us.

And the bramble said unto the trees, If in truth ye anoint me king over you, then come and put your trust in my shadow: and if not, let fire come out of the bramble and devour the cedars of Lebanon.

Now therefore, if ye have done truly and sincerely, in that ye have made Abimelech king, and if ye have dealt well with Jerubbaal and his house, and have done unto him according to the deserving of his hands;

(For my father fought for you, and adventured his life far, and delivered you out of the hands of Midian;

And ye are risen up against my father's house this day, and have slain his sons, threescore and ten persons, upon one stone, and have made Abimelech, the son of his maidservant, king over the men of Shechem, because he is your brother;)

If ye then have dealt truly and sincerely with Jerubbaal and with his house this day, then rejoice ye in Abimelech, and let him also rejoice in you:

But if not, let fire come out from Abimelech, and devour the men of Shechem, and the house of Millo; and let fire come out from the men of Shechem, and from the house of Millo, and devour Abimelech. (Judges 9:8:20).

GIDEON A TRUE STATESMAN

The country was in sore distress, overrun by the accursed Midianites. The people had called to God in their adversity and He planned another great deliverance for them. Gideon was spoken to and enlisted after many doubts and testings. Overthrowing the Baal altars, built by his father, he showed his courage as well as his faith in the outcome of the scheme. It raised a great disturbance, but placed Baal on the defensive and he went down amid the pleadings of his disillusioned followers. Truth fears no exposures; the noonday sun is its native air.

Gideon's trumpet call produced one-sixth of Israel only; five-sixths remained at home through fear, ridicule, indifference or entangling alliances. Thirty-two thousand arrived who were willing, but after seeing the young farmer prophet and hearing his voice and understanding their task, twenty-two thousand went back, declaring it could not be done. Of the ten thousand remaining nine thousand seven hundred were found to be too lazy or slow to get anywhere. This left three hundred willing, courageous, enthusiastic followers. They were or-

JOTHAM'S PARABLE

ganized, they were equipped, they obeyed orders: the battle was won and Israel was saved!

How refreshing it is to see Gideon declining political preferment, and when asked to be their ruler and establish through his family a line of kings, he said, "I will not rule over you, neither shall my sons rule over you; the Lord shall rule over you." (Judges 8:23.) So Gideon went back to his humble home and lived and died in private ranks. The one bad thing that Gideon ever did, however, was the cause of his family's downfall. "And his concubine that was in Shechem, she also bare him a son whose name he called Abimelech." For, after Gideon's death, Abimelech, this son by his maid servant, stirred up the people to place him in power. In his mad ambition to gain authority he murdered his sixty-nine half-brothers. Jotham alone escaped and gives to us this wonderful parable which has a modern application as well as an ancient.

THE RULING OLIVE

"But the olive tree said unto them, should I leave my fatness, wherewith by me they honor God and man, and go to be promoted over the trees?"

Men of today crave material wealth as king of their lives. Bradstreet out rates God's street, with many. Money is not to be despised. For proper use it is to be desired. "Diligent in business, fervent in spirit, serving the Lord," is the right attitude. Success is the bride of endeavor. Slothfulness hath no virtue. Work is ennobling. All great men have been great workers. Idleness breeds crime. Make your money serve humanity and heaven, and do not let it curse you, as it did Harry Thaw, Loeb and Leopold, the rich young ruler, Judas Iscariot, Dives and the famous barn builder. With many today character without cash is shabby gentility. They live by the rule of gold and not by the golden rule. The olive is emperor of their lives.

SUGAR IS KING

"But the fig tree said unto them, should I forsake my sweetness, and my good fruit, and go to be promoted over the trees?"

Many people today are begging for the sweets of life to the exclusion of the substantials. Some sugar is necessary, but in making the human body God put more salt into it than sugar. There are some pastors and evangelists who are just too sweet for anything. They never correct or warn, but just pass the sugar bowl. Their effort seems to be to humanize God, deify man and minify sin. This is an ice-cream-soda day. Can you imagine John the Baptist being one of this type? Every fiber of this old trail-blazer and pathfinder would have revolted against such a policy. Listen to him: "Ye generation of vipers, who hath warned you to flee from the wrath to come?" See him point his finger at Herod while he reads the riot act concerning his dirty life with his niece. No fig juice in this! He was imprisoned and beheaded, but he left a record that modern preachers would do well to emulate. Listen to Jesus in language that almost scorches the paper as He denounces the blindness and hypocracy of the scribes and Pharisees: "Ye serpents, ye generation of vipers, how can you escape the damnation of hell!" Paul was accused of turning the world upside down, he was beaten with rods, cut with stones and beheaded on Nero's block, but his was no lolly pop message. We have too much of the fig tree attitude in our churches, our homes, our schools and the world today. That is one reason why our jails and penitentiaries are crowded. Don't let the fig tree reign in your life. Use it for dessert, but not for the main ration.

PLEASURE REIGNS

"And the vine said unto them, should I leave my wine, which cheereth God and man, and go to be promoted over the trees?"

The cry of the world is for license. Let us alone, cry the young people. It is the cry of personal error, organized crime and a back-slidden church and a God-defying day. Let us have a good time. We hear it everywhere. The pastors are kings without kingdoms. Parents no longer consult them about their children's pleasures, education or morals. Parents have abdicated their God-ordained throne of authority to their children. God cursed Eli for not controlling his family and commended Abraham for commanding his. Joshua said, "As for me and my house we will serve the Lord."

Take the modern dance. It is heathen in origin, animalistic in action, devilish in results. It is a divorce feeder, a church emptier and a spiritual paralyzer. But it has swept the swinging, singing

teens from the church by the millions. To oppose
it is to be censured and abused. This is peculiarly a day of amusement. The dance halls and bathing beaches and picture palaces are crowded day
and night. Sensual books and magazines glut our
stands and stores. To raise a voice against them is
but to advertise them. Smoking, drinking and cutting the hair like a man has coarsened the modern
woman and is fast cheapening her. Bobbed hair is
just one more part of the modern slump of the
modern woman. The cigarette habit is a growing
menace among women and is a sign of womanly decadence, and also one of the causes of the increased
death rate from tuberculosis. Preachers and
parents alike seem helpless before this modern juggernaut of pleasure. Let the vine reign over us,
the many millions cry today.

THE ENTHRONEMENT OF THE BRIAR

"And the bramble said unto the trees, if in
truth you anoint me king over you, then come
put your trust in my shadow: and if not let fire
come out of the bramble and devour the cedars of
Lebanon."

This is a bramble age and day. The bramble
has reigned through all the centuries in many hearts
and lives. Ahab and Jezebel were ruled by the
bramble of covetousness. Elisha's servant also
bowed to this throne. Eve let the briar of eye-lust
entangle her. Achan put his trust in the bramble's
shadow when he stole the Babylonian garment and
golden wedge. King David surrendered his throne

and seated the bramble when he kidnaped Uriah's wife and murdered her husband. The bramble today is reigning in governors' chairs and ruling on judges' benches, sitting in senate chambers and legislative halls, as well as in the homes of the lowly. The bramble of avarice, the bramble of hate, the bramble of profanity, the bramble of impurity grows in every land and clime, burning, scratching and bleeding the people.

You are familiar with the outcome of this sad story. Jotham's prophecy came true, for Abemilech was a briar indeed and bled the people. While he killed sixty-nine of his half-brothers on a rock, he himself was killed by a rock in the hands of a woman. Thus he perished, reaping what he had sown, reaping the kind he had sown and reaping more than he had sown, forcing others after him also to reap his harvest of iniquity.

THE OLD OAK STANDS AMID THE STORM

One summer afternoon my wife and I were sitting on our front porch, watching the neighborhood children play 'neath the foliage of a gigantic oak tree in our front yard. A great grass rope swing, attached to one of its noble limbs, afforded the children much delight, as they would pump and swing, letting the old cat die. We had become very much attached to the tree. In fact, on embarking on my many pilgrimages to distant fields where I labored as an evangelist, I would often pause long enough to caress its bark and leave my family in its charge. Upon my return I always saluted it first. It must have been a pretty big bush when Abraham came out of Ur of the Chaldees. As we sat there we saw a cloud forming in the west, over the river. It soon assumed cyclonic proportions. The sky was darkened. My wife said, "Burke,. let's go to the basement; I am afraid." Just then the wind struck. Fences were blown down, garages turned over and a big glass in the front room smashed, while the porch furniture was swept into the yard. As my wife ran to the basement with the children, I hugged a column on the porch, and watched the glory of the storm. As lightnings flashed and thunders boomed the grand old tree engaged the storm. Bending and swaying to and fro, it looked as if its trunk would be snapped near the ground. Roots were leaving the ground, leaves were falling from its boughs and in my anxiety I cried out, "Good-bye old tree, good-bye!" But the old tree seemed to gather up its strength, straightened itself and fought on. The storm soon swept by, and after the rain came the sun, and from a thousand leaves on the good old tree diamonds were hanging, and on the topmost limb a little "Bill Shakespeare" was tearing off a strip. Walking into the yard I said, "Old tree, you have taught me a lesson. When the storms of life are beating upon Jesus Christ, His church and His Word, upon the home and the school, like yourself I want to fight and be able to stand in the face of the squalls of hell, sinking my roots deeper into the 'faith of our fathers.'"

JOTHAM'S PARABLE

There is a legend which tells us that it was of aspen wood that the cross upon which Jesus Christ died was made, and that is why the aspen trembles so when you approach it, seeming to be conscious of the humiliation that it was put to. We are told that when Jesus rode through Jerusalem branches from the palm trees were cut and waved toward Him, as the multitude cried, "Hail! Hail!" The palm symbolizes victory—victory over sin, death and the grave. Strange it was from a tree Eve took the forbidden fruit, and it was upon a tree that Christ died for you and for me. Listen to Sidney Lanier:

> Into the woods my Master went,
> Clean forspent, forspent;
> Into the woods my Master came,
> Forspent with love and shame.
> But the olives they were not blind to Him,
> The little gray leaves were kind to Him,
> The thorn tree had a mind for Him,
> When into the woods He came.
>
> Out of the woods my Master went,
> And He was well content;
> Out of the woods my Master came,
> Content with death and shame.
> When death and shame would woo Him last,
> From under the trees they drew Him last,
> 'Twas on a tree they slew Him—last,
> When out of the woods He came."

CHAPTER III.

THE INCARNATION

For God so loved the world that He gave His only begotten Son, that whosoever believeth in Him should not perish, but have everlasting life. (John 3:16).

The mystery of the incarnation is the credential of the divinity of our religion. God-made things are often both mysterious and wonderful. Take the bird's wing, composed of over a million barbs and barblets, each turning upon its axis so that the upstroke of the wing lets the air through and the downward stroke makes the wings impervious to it, and each barblet is built up of thousands of cells, producing the exact strength, elasticity and cohesion of the whole. I cannot understand the power of sleep which takes me into oblivion and returns me invigorated for the day's task. I do not understand the stars, the wind, the light, but I stand under them and enjoy them. I do not know why acids eat you, rocks crush you, fire burns you, but I have learned they do.

The word incarnation is the mightiest word in the lexicon of heaven or earth, and a word often misunderstood. I doubt not the lightnings flashed and shimmered as much in Adam's day as in ours, but we had to await the coming of a man with kite, bottle and string. We never see an electric bulb or telegraph wire or cablegram or radio that the wonder of it does not call up Franklin, Edison, Marconi or Morse. These great toilers, diggers, delvers, thinkers, have placed their brain, blood and muscle and very lives into the study of the ether waves that mankind might be blessed. But this is not incarnation. Take the laughing, leaping Niagara, worth many times over to be sure the tourist's ticket and time to go and behold its reflected and refracted beauty, but it was at best only a spill of nature or waste of energy. But a man came along and harnessed this great power, and today Niagara turns ponderous machinery, lights distant cities, and in many ways blesses the world. But this is not incarnation.

Luther Burbank, the wizard of the vegetable world, has redeemed many wild flowers to our wedding marches and bridal altars. He has caused the cactus to drop its spines. He will make the desert blossom as the rose. He has produced the thornless rose before the ministers could show a sinless world, or the doctors a painless planet. In new creations of fruit, flowers and berries, by budding and grafting, he has left a name to endure forever. Yet this is not incarnation.

Someone has said that a diamond is a congealed sunbeam, that the sunbeam, under pressure and heat, has imbedded itself in the anthracite or charcoal. Thus we have the diamond—the common coal kissed and lifted by the sun to the realm of love, courtship and marriage. Still this is not incarnation. Again, we find the bivalve in the depth of the sea. A grain of sand in its shell, producing pain, causes it to make an effort to segregate this particle of sand and, in the effort, a pearl is formed. Here we have life, suffering and death—the pearl. Jesus likens the kingdom of heaven to a pearl of great price. (Matthew 13:46).

Here are a young man and woman, both healthy and bubbling over with life, love, ambition and hope. They marry and move away to themselves, leaving their "in-laws," (and outlaws) according to God's plan. After several years a little stranger visits them. That's her baby! No, it's his baby! No, it's their baby! Love, sympathy, sacrifice, potential death of their potential death. A new creature partaking of both father and mother natures. He has his mother's eyes and his daddy's mouth. Each day the fond parents find some likeness to themselves in their own darling child. This is human incarnation. Congenital tendencies and natural impartations of both parents are found in the new-born babe.

God made Adam and Eve and placed them in Edenic environment. God was a spirit and they were flesh. They left God and His garden, but through every singing bird and babbling brook and blooming flower God declared his love for them. Their descendants multiplied. Failing to hold their love through spiritual ministry and angelic warning and voice of nature, He sought them again by selecting the best He could find among them, calling them to be prophets and priests, and inspiring them he sent them out to call man back. But man in his wickedness, stoned these prophets and killed these preachers, and down the highway of life rushed on rampant, finding new pleasures in sin until God in holy desperation and love said, "I will win him back. He must love me again. I will go down in bodily form and walk the ways of men. I will be born down that I may lift man up." But how can the infinite God come into finite man? How can the eternal be compressed into the temporal? Science is today showing us many transformations which may, by analogy, throw some light on this the pivotal scheme of man's redemption.

THE LAW OF ENVIRONMENT AND REFINEMENT

I am told that the Chinese can take a yellow canary, put it with its mate in a white cage, in a white room, attended by a white-garbed attendant, feed it white food and in three generations produce a snow white bird. If you will turn to Genesis 30:35 you will find that Jacob knew the value of environment in stock breeding, and had mastered its secrets to the confusion of his father-in-law and the enrichment of his own purse.

While the law of environment is a great one, the art of refining the blood of horses, cows, dogs, chickens, hogs is still more miraculous. Lou Dillon, Nancy Hanks, Black and Gold, My Own, Zev and other thoroughbred horses, well known in the sporting pages of the world's newspapers, are common horses whose blood was so carefully guarded that they were born to the purple. We no longer have the old-fashioned domineck, blue and sooty hen, but instead we have the white Orpingtons, Rhode Island Reds, Anconas, Barred Plymouth Rocks. To go through the poultry department of any state fair is but to witness the fact that men have been able to change color, quality and nature in the fowl kingdom. When I was a boy there were hogs that could eat slop out of a lead pipe; they were called "razor backs." But today we have the Durocs and other fine strains with scarcely any nose at all, literally rolling in fat. ready for the packing houses. There are cows today that produce twelve and fifteen gallons of milk per day—Jerseys and Holsteins—while their ancestresses would produce scarcely three gallons per day. A man presented me with a blooded pointer pup, declaring that his daddy's, daddy's, daddy's daddy and his mother's, mother's, mother's mother were thoroughbreds, blue-ribboners and prize-winners; that every drop of blood in this pup was regal, purple. I took him home, and one cold, autumnal morning I whistled for him and he came bounding from the kennel. I said to him, "They tell me you never smelled a bird or heard a gun bark, but your forebears for four generations on each side have thrilled to the call of old Bob White, and have held many covies for the gunners to shoot. It's up to you to prove your blood; let's go." I've never seen a dog of mature years range as well and wide as this six month's old pup did. After thirty minutes of chase

THE INCARNATION

I whistled him in. With wagging tail, lolling tongue and dancing eye he seemed to say "I am having the time of my life." Rewarding him with a pat on the head and small piece of bread I directed him to another field. He leaped forward and was gone. I followed, but was soon out-distanced. He failing to return to me I called him long and loud, but no response. I thought possibly he had gone home, but going a few hundred yards farther I came upon him in an open space, standing before a pile of brush, his left foot raised, his head turned sideways, his tail taut and straight, his eyes blazing. He was gently whining, and his very posture seemed to say, "Make haste, master, come on. I don't know what it is, but right here in front of me I feel the call of my forebearers' blood; I can't stand it much longer." I said, "Steady, steady; hold 'em, Jack, hold 'em." He held them until I walked up by him and kicked the brush, and as the covey took the air I fired twice and—missed! I'll never forget the look the dog gave me. It seemed to say, "If you'd been as much of a thoroughbred as I am you would have brought down three of those birds." On the way home he acted as if he had the edge on me when it came to blood.

When we see what man, by environment and breeding, has done with animals, we are not surprised at what God would be able to accomplish by guarding the blood through Abraham and Sarah, Rebecca and Isaac, Jacob and Rachael and on down until we come to that most marvelous of all women

—Mary, the mother of Christ. In Genesis 3:15 we read that the woman's seed should bruise the serpent's head. Elsewhere in nature it is the seed of the male, but it seems to me in this scripture the virgin-born Son of God was foretold.

There is sex in all vegetable life. On every bush and tree you will find this is true. Some magisterial wind or priestly butterfly performs the marriage ceremony and flowers and fruit are the children of these botanical unions. There is not a molecule or atom or electron or proton that does not come into life through the mystic gateway of birth. We are told by the astronomers that this same law holds good in the kingdom of the stars. Then if in the ponderosity of planets and the minutiae of electrons, as well as in the human, vegetable and animal kingdoms, each realm is peopled through the mystic gateway of birth, why should not God use this same route when the White Priest of eternity would walk the ways of man? The little flower-visiting, honey-gathering bee has been given the power of determining sex. A certain food is fed, producing males; another females, another neuter, or working bees. The queen bee puts on her bridal veil and selects from a number of male bees her mate. These prospective bridegrooms have been set apart, awaiting the time when she should come, and when her choice is made their bridal tour is through the blue skies above them, and in the afternoon at tawny dusk, when the evening stars their prayers have said, the

THE INCARNATION

bride-groom falls back to earth intoxicated with love and dies. The queen bee lays hundreds of eggs daily as long as she lives. These eggs are taken out by the working bees, sunned and fed, and their sex determined, as necessity demands. I say if God has thus endowed the little busy, honey-making bee, could not the Holy Ghost overshadow a pure virgin? And echo answers, "Why not?"

FOR GOD SO LOVED THE WORLD.

God's love was perfect. Mary's love was humanly perfect. When the angel of the annunciation came to her and told his mission her reply was beautiful. The story of the angelic visitation is a direct statement of God's modus operandi in reaching man. When He had prepared a human medium through which He would come, He commissioned Gabriel to tell Mary of his purpose. (Luke 1:26-35.) "And in the sixth month the angel Gabriel was sent from God unto a city of Galilee, named Nazareth, to a virgin espoused to a man whose name was Joseph, of the house of David; and the virgin's name was Mary. And the angel came unto her, and said, 'Hail, thou that art highly favoured, the Lord is with thee: blessed art thou among women.' And when she saw him, she was troubled at his saying, and cast about in her mind what manner of salutation this should be. And the angel said unto her, 'Fear not, Mary, for thou hast found favor with God. And behold, thou shalt conceive in thy womb, and bring forth a son, and shalt call his name JESUS. He shall be great, and shall be called the

Son of the Highest: and the Lord God shall give unto him the throne of his father David: And he shall reign over the house of Jacob forever; and of his kingdom there shall be no end.' Then said Mary unto the angel, 'How shall this be, seeing I know not a man?' And the angel answered and said unto her, 'The Holy Ghost shall come upon thee, and the power of the Highest shall overshadow thee: therefore also that holy thing which shall be born of thee shall be called the Son of God.' "

Tradition tells us that Mary often served in the temple, washing pots and scrubbing floors and polishing the holy vessels, and that for hours she would stand and gaze at the beauty of the sanctuary. Her reply to Gabriel and her actions afterward showed her love for God and her precocity in things divine. No wonder Jesus was lovely; he was a love child on the earth's side as well as heaven's. God so loved the world that He gave His only begotten Son. Mary so loved God that she gave her Son to the world.

It is said by someone that Jesus challenges the attention of the world by His many-sidedness. He meets the needs of all classes and conditions of men. As deep answereth unto deep, so does He respond to the movings of each soul of man.

"Call the roll of the world's workers and ask, 'What think ye of Christ?' Their answers amaze us by their revelation of this many-sidedness of our Lord.

"To the artist He is the One Altogether Lovely. To the architect He is the Chief Corner Stone. To

THE INCARNATION 53

the astronomer He is the Sun of Righteousness. To the baker He is the Bread of Life. To the banker He is the Hid Treasure. To the biologist He is the Life. To the builder He is the Sure Foundation. To the carpenter He is the Door. To the doctor He is the Great Physician. To the educator He is the Great Teacher. To the farmer He is the Sower, and the Lord of the Harvest. To the Florist He is the Rose of Sharon and the Lily of the Valley. To the geologist He is the Rock of Ages. To the horticulturist He is the True Vine. To the judge He is the Righteous Judge, the Judge of All Men. To the juror He is the Faithful and True Witness. To the jeweler He is the Pearl of Great Price. To the lawyer He is the Counselor, the Lawgiver, the Advocate. To the newspaper man He is the Good Tidings of Great Joy. To the oculist He is the Light of the Eyes. To the philanthropist He is the Unspeakable Gift. To the philosopher He is the Wisdom of God. To the preacher He is the Word of God. To the railroad man He is the New and Living Way. To the sculptor He is the Living Stone. To the servant He is the Good Master. To the statesman He is the Desire of All Nations. To the student He is the Incarnate Truth. To the theologian He is the Author and Finisher of Our Faith. To the toiler He is the Giver of Rest. To the sinner He is the Lamb of God, which taketh away the sin of the world. To the christian He is the Son of the Living God, the Savior, Redeemer and Lord. What is He to you?" Napoleon called Jesus the Emperor of Love. What a title! What a kingdom! What an Emperor!

One of the finest illustrations of Christ the world has ever known is found in the "Christ and the Cross of the Andes:"

"Argentina and Chile are separated by the Andes mountains, which are so high that their summits are always covered with snow. A dispute arose between the two countries as to the exact boundary line up there on the mountains. They quarreled over it in hot Spanish words. Then they began to get ready to fight over it by building guns and warships and drilling their soldiers. But the women did not want war. Through the efforts of two leading bishops and these women, the leaders finally agreed to submit the question to Queen Victoria, of England, for arbitration and a treaty of peace was signed on May 28, 1903.

"In the meantime a young Argentine sculptor had made a beautiful bronze statue of Christ from cannons taken during the war of Independence with Spain. Senora de Costa, on the day the treaty was signed, invited the Argentine president and Chile's representative to inspect this statue and asked permission to have it placed on a high pass of the Andes, as a symbol of perpetual peace between Argentina and Chile. This was done, at a cost of $100,000. There it stands amid the eternal snows, teaching the whole world a noble lesson. On its granite base are carved the words: 'Sooner shall these mountains crumble to dust than Argentine's

THE INCARNATION

and Chilean's break the peace which at the feet of Christ the Redeemer they have sworn to maintain.'"

Edward Markham, the American poet, author of "The Man With the Hoe," wrote the following poem on "The Christ of the Andes:"

>Where once of old wild battles roared,
>And brother-blood was on the sword;
>Now all the fields are rich wilth grain
>And roses redden all the plain.
>
>Torn were the peoples with feuds and hates
>Fear on the mountain-walls, death at the gates:
>Then through the clamor of arms was heard
>A whisper of the Master's word.
>
>'Fling down your swords: be friends again:
>Ye are not wolf-packs: ye are men.
>Let brother-counsel be the law:
>Not serpent fang, not tiger claw.'
>
>Chile and Argentina heard;
>Then great hopes in their spirits stirred;
>The red swords from their clenched fists fell,
>And heaven shone out where once was hell!
>
>"They hurled their cannons into flame
>And out of the forge the strong Christ came.
>'Twas thus they molded in happy fire
>The tall Christ of their hearts' desire.
>
>O Christ of Olivet, you hushed the wars
>Under the far Andean stars:
>Lift now your strong nail-wounded hands
>Over all peoples, over all lands—
>Stretch out those comrade hands to be
>A shelter over land and sea!

Pilate called Him the faultless one. There isn't a perfect flower in all the world, nor is there a perfect man or bird or beast. Jesus is the only perfect one whoever trod the ways of man. Sidney Lanier so beautifully sings of Him:

> But Thee, but Thee, O Sovereign seer of time,
> But thee, O poet's wisdom's tongue.
> But The, O man's best man, O love's best love,
> O perfect life, in perfect labor writ,
> Of all men comrade, servant, king and priest.
> What if, or yet, what more, what flaw, what lapse,
> What least defect or shadow of defect,
> What rumor tattled by an enemy,
> Of inference loose, what lack of grace,
> Even in torture's grasp or sleep's or death's,—
> O what amiss may I forgive in Thee,
> Jesus, good paragon, Thou Crystal Christ?

FOR GOD SO SYMPATHIZED WITH THE WORLD

God in sympathy gave His only begotten Son, and Mary so sympathized with God that she was willing to give her Son. Intelligent sympathy means a fellow feeling. Unless you have suffered likewise, you may feel sorry for the sufferer, but you cannot really sympathize with him. Jesus went where the blind were blundering, where the lepers were loathed, where the friendless were forgotten, where the poor were pushed to the wall, where the magdalenas were maltreated. Because it was His people, His blood, He loved them, He sympathized with them. I have known the father whose child was epileptic to hold that child while in the throes of the spasm. The parent would grit his teeth and roll his eyes and froth at the mouth just like the unfortunate victim, and when the fit had left the little one limp of body and idiotic of expression, I have seen the father wipe the froth from the child's face and then from his own and have heard him say, "Oh. God, spare my child, set her free, let me bear it all!" Jesus was in such sympathy with us that he

THE INCARNATION

suffered for us. Paul also declares he could wish himself accursed for his brethren's sake, so fully had he caught the spirit of Christ, the Christ of sympathy. "For we have not a high priest which cannot be touched with the feeling of our infirmities; but was in all points tempted like as we are, yet without sin. Let us therefore come boldly unto the throne of grace that we may obtain mercy and find grace to help in time of need."

FOR GOD SO SACRIFICED FOR THE WORLD

He gave His only begotten Son, and Mary so sacrificed for God that she gave her Son, her happiness, her good name, that the world through her Son might be saved. God's love and sympathy are measured by his sacrifice and sympathy for us in giving His only Son to die the death of a felon on the despised cross. If we value God's gift by its cost, it is impossible to tabulate its worth, for it robbed God and heaven and forever branded Mary as shameless in the eyes of the world.

We have seen a young wife give to her husband the roses of her body and the lilies of her mind; yea, we have seen her go down into the depths that defy the fathom lines of science and philosophy. We have seen her go out into no-man's land, where angels' wings have never flown, and out there meet God and take from Him a precious little immortal and bring it back to train for heaven. A woman's sacrifice is the only earthly thing that would even faintly illustrate the great sacrifice of God. A woman gives all to her husband, her children.

No painter's brush or poet's pen,
  In justice to her fame,
Has ever reached half high enough
  To write the mother's name.

Make ink of tears and molten gems,
  And sunbeams mixed together,
With holy hand and golden pen,
  Go write the name of mother.

In every humble tenant's house,
  In every cottage home,
In marble courts and gilded halls
  On every palace dome;

On mountains high, in valleys low,
  In every land and clime,
On every throbbing human heart
  That blessed name enshrine.

Take childhood's light and manhood's shade,
  Celestial canvas given,
In beauty trace that name and face
  And hang it up in heaven.

High up above the towering mount,
  Beyond the starry skies,
Write it on every glittering crown
  That's worn in paradise.

Thence upward to the great white throne,
  'Midst music soft and sweet,
Thank Jesus for your mother's name,
  And write it at His feet.*

FOR GOD SO DIED FOR THE WORLD

And when they were come to the place called Calvary, there they crucified Him, and the malefactors, one on the right hand, and the other on the left.

Then said Jesus: "Father forgive them, for they know not what they do. (Luke 23:4, 35).

If you will read from Matthew, Mark and John you will find that, after the most unfair trial ever given, the circumstances of the death of Christ were most exasperating. The world was there; His trial

---
*Selected

THE INCARNATION

had attracted as had His life. The miracle worker had been apprehended. Rumor said he had been proved guilty of treason. His friends had all fled, except a few women. He had failed to make good His claims as rightful heir to any throne. Many were present who had been the recipients of His healing touch, or munificent bounty, but all mouths which could open in His defense were closed, but one. The company in which He had been led to His doom, two thieves, was a sufficient commentary on what the custodians of law and liberty thought. The moving throng had caught the rumor from the verdict of Pilate, and the Jews, and wagged their heads and said, "Thou that destroyest the temple and buildest it in three days, *save Thyself, and come down from the cross.*" Likewise the chief priests said among themselves with the scribes, "He saved others, Himself He cannot save." And one of the malefactors railed on Him. The soldiers mocked Him. The women looked on from afar. The gamblers for His clothing were indifferent to His sufferings. A Centurion said a kind word, but He was dead and heard it not. The people looked on while nature was in convulsion. God had hidden His face. Under these circumstances this prayer was uttered. High politics, mammon, envy, anger, and jealousy all played a part in the death of Jesus. They were time servers. They were a mob. They were a trust of iniquity. They were all ignorant. The argument in Christ's prayer was that they were ignorant, or, at least, partially so. Peter, on the day of Pentecost, after that terrific charge, said, "But I wot that ye did it ignorantly." Paul said he got pardon for his sins, because he did it through ignorance. Just what did He mean by saying, "They know not what they do?" If ignorance is some excuse, can you plead it? His murderers had only three short years to study Him and His claims. You have had nearly two thousand years. Are you ignorant of His resurrection, and that He made good his every claim? Are you ignorant of the success which has attended the preaching of the gospel? Have you not seen every other system pale before the doctrines which He taught? Has not your home, some man or woman you know, your own conscience, borne witness to you of the divinity of Christ, and the need of the salvation which He offers?

Yes, He loved, He sympathized, He sacrificed, He died for you and me. He was the world's greatest philosopher, the world's greatest orator, the world's greatest controversalist, the world's only regal strategist, and the world's only transformer. Napoleon, Charlemagne, Caesar and all other great warriors have said to their men, "Die for me," but Jesus said, "I'll die for you." He reversed the order. For God so loved the world that He died through His Son that whosoever believeth in Him should not die but have everlasting life, "Nature forms us, sin deforms us, schools inform us, preachers reform us," but the loving, sympathizing, sacrificing, dying Son of God transforms us.

THE INCARNATION

All hail the power of Jesus' name,
  Let angels prostrate fall,
Bring forth the royal diadem
And crown Him Lord of all.

Ye chosen seed of Israel's race,
  Ye ransomed from the fall,
Hail Him who saves you by His grace,
And crown Him Lord of all.

Sinners whose love can ne'er forget
  The wormwood and the gall,
Go spread your trophies at His feet,
And crown Him Lord of all.

Let every kindred, every tribe,
  On this terrestrial ball,
To Him all majesty ascribe,
And crown Him Lord of all.

Oh, that with yonder sacred throng,
  We at His feet may fall,
We'll join the everlasting song,
And crown Him Lord of all.

CHAPTER IV.

IMMORTALITY

For what shall it profit a man if he gain the whole world and lose his own soul, or what shall a man give in exchange for his soul? (Mark 8:36).

> The soul of man, Jehovah's breath,
> That keeps two worlds at strife,
> Hell moves beneath to work its death,
> Heaven stoops to give it life.

DIVINE AND HUMAN ESTIMATES OF LIFE AND SOUL

Man is a tri-partite being—body, mind and soul—and I wish to discuss with you the soul, that part of man that will live when the world is on fire. Yea, when the sun is turned into midnight darkness, the moon into blood and the stars like untimely fruit have dropped to the ground. I do not predicate immortality of regeneration, but of creation. Neither do I believe the soul to be a mere secretion, or immortality an award for righteous living. God made man and then breathed into him the breath of lives, so whether you are good or bad, right or wrong, you will live forever somewhere—either with Moses and the Lamb or Dives and the damned. You can see God's estimate of life in how he has created it. He seems to have spilled life with a prodigal hand. Life in the air, water, in fact, everywhere. A drop of water hanging to your finger has often within it

IMMORTALITY

multiplied millions of forms of life. God's estimate of life can be seen not only in its abundant creation, but in the natural instinct for the preservation of life which is in all animal, human and vegetable creatures. God seems to have made life under a recuperative law. Cut your hand and nature will try to heal it; scar the trees, and the bark will come again. There is in everything a love of life and a corresponding fear of death. You may ride a horse up to an engine or automobile; unafraid he will stand there, but ride him up into the presence of a dead horse and he will tremble beneath you. Often when cows are driven to the cattle yard, they lift a bovine wail in protest to the God of life against the shedding of the blood of their kind. God has furthermore said to man, "Thou shalt not kill," and "He that sheddeth man's blood by man shall his blood be shed," which is a divine protection of the life of mankind.

You can see man's estimate of life by the way he abuses it. Liquor, lust, dissipation, war, tobacco and a thousand other forms of destruction are today preying upon man's life; all of which goes to show man's appreciation or lack of appreciation of this God-given treasure. You can see God's estimate of the soul by what he has done for it in the gift of the bible, the Sabbath day, the church, the Son of God, the Holy Spirit—all for man's soul. You can often see how man undervalues his soul by the way he neglects these means of grace which God has so freely given.

IMMORTALITY UNQUESTIONED IN SOME OF THE LOWER FORMS OF LIFE

Dr. Paul Carus, in a little booklet, "Whence and Whither," has said: "Death does not exist in the realm of the lowly organized beings. Amoebas and moners grow and divide, they do not die. The mother breaks up into two daughters, but leaves no corpse behind, for the daughters are identical in structure as well as substance with the mother. If thus immortality be the natural state of life on its lowest scale, how is it that death appears with the rise of higher forms of life? Is not death perhaps a factor in the life which is subservient to a purpose that works for good? Such in fact is the case. Death appears in the scale of life as the necessary concomitant of individuality, and individuality originates with birth. Some polyps, and among them corals, multiply by division. Every moner, every polyp thus produced starts in life as a full fledged creature. There is no state of infancy, with all of its troubles and dangers, to be passed through, for the creatures make their first appearance in a state of maturity." If death be unknown in these lower forms of life, it should certainly be unfeared in the higher realm of mankind. God would not give to these creatures of low estate the precious gift of immortality and deny it to the sons of men, who are made in His image. The universal consent of mankind to the hope of immortality has been recognized in all ages from the beginning.

I do not argue the immortality of the soul

IMMORTALITY

through love, fear, dreams, memory, grief or power to assemble. Everything loves. The dog loves his master, the cow her calf, the mare her colt, the husband his wife, the mother her children. This is the natural instinct. I do not base much faith in dreams. I have known a dog to be lying on the porch asleep, and dreaming that he was in the chase he would bark and then arise and look shamefaced and lie down again. His bark indicated he was under full cry for some red fox, and when awakened, disappointment was in his eye. I once had a little pet bantam hen that dreamed she was a rooster and crowed, but that did not make her one. You can eat a lot of corned beef and cabbage, drink strong coffee, lie down in a hot room and your dreams will not be pleasant; but with the proper diet and a well ventilated room, with the south wind blowing on you, you may sleep and dream that life is beautiful. I do not base my belief in immortality on grief. I have known some dogs to grieve longer over their master's grave than some widows over their husband's death. The wood pigeon of Egypt is black. It never re-mates. Where its mate was last seen it sits and coos and coos its life away. Tertullian tells us this is where mourning comes from. Grief will not often kill; if it did, there is many a mother who would be dead through grief over her wayward boys. I do not base my belief in immortality on the fact that man is a great assembler. Man creates nothing, but he assembles much. He assembled the steam engine, the radio, the typewriter, the automobile, our great skyscrapers. In fact, all progress is due to this skill of man; but man created none of the materials with which he has worked. I have several reasons to offer in support of the doctrine of the immortality of man's soul.

MAN HAS A CONSCIENCE

He is the only earthly creature capable of operating in the moral kingdom. He alone of all created life has a conscience, and a sense of responsibility.

The abolition of slavery, the outlawry of liquor, the liberation of woman, the welfare of children, the recognition of the laboring man, the building of churches, hospitals and colleges, all for the uplift of mankind, show him to be more than a mere animal. He seems happiest when working for the amelioration of the down-trodden and discouraged ones of earth. He is constantly showing his kinship with God.

PROGRESSIVE IN NATURE

Progress in every earthly realm, save the human, is slow, tortuous, indefinite. Its records are clocked by the tick of ages. The blue bird builds its nest in the same way its ancestors did a thousand years ago. Wild geese continue to fly north in the summer and south in the winter; they have never found a better way. The little squirrels house their nuts in the holes of the trees, just as they did in the beginning. But when you come to the kingdom of man, you find him ever reaching up, he is never satisfied; he is demanding better modes of conveyance, better working conditions, better houses, better roads, better schools, better churches, and more direct means of communication. A man of the twentieth century would not go back to the ox cart for any consideration, or to tallow candles, dirt roads or log cabins. He demands something better each generation. Did you ever take a Florida orange, golden and sweet, and suck it until every drop had been extracted, and then hurl it down and reach for another? Man has taken the gold and silver and coal and diamonds, the oil —in fact, man has just about sucked this golden earth dry. God must have some other place for man to occupy soon, for he has about exhausted this little world. There will soon be as many airships flying in the air as there are automobiles upon the earth. With radio and gasoline and airships, man is getting ready for other splendid adventures. There is a restlessness in him which this world cannot satisfy. He is innately progressive. He is now arranging schedules and time tables for other worlds. He has found Mars to be thirty-seven million miles from earth, while Saturn is only seven hundred and fifty million miles away. With his powerful telescopes he has swept out into the spiral nebulæ some sixty billion miles, finding new worlds all the time, and the end is not yet.

INFINITE IN CAPACITY

Anything that is finite in capacity is finite in nature, and anything that is infinite in capacity is infinite in nature. Light is food for the eye, but you can give the eye so much light as to blind it. You can give the ear so much sound that it will burst. You can give your stomach too much food and too much water. Your eye, ear and stomach are finite in capacity; therefore they are finite in nature, and therefore will perish. But you never hear of a human soul unable to assimilate truth. You cannot give the soul too much of God. The soul is infinite in capacity, therefore it must be infinite in nature, and if it is infinite in nature only an infinite God can satisfy it. It is scientifically true, so I am told, that no effect can be greater than the cause; that no stream can rise higher than its source; that there can be no faculty without function. If this be true, then when I see what man has done, is doing and can do, I know that only God is the cause that brought the soul into existence; and as I see the stream of civilization rising higher and higher, I am thoroughly convinced that its source is in God. When I remember that man has a faculty for worship and praise, I know that somewhere, sometime this faculty must function, in adoration to God or in bitter remorse, for man is infinite in capacity, therefore, he must be infinite in nature.

IMMORTAL IN DESIRE

Men long to live. There is no appetite or passion stronger than the desire for immortality. We have pictures taken that we may live on in the memory of our loved ones. We build monuments of brick and stone and write books in order that we may not be forgotten, that the unborn of earth may read the books and see the monuments. Man never leaves a finished picture on the easel. He hopes somewhere in a nightless world to work on forever. I sometimes get hungry, but there is food for my body which God provides. There is the cold, thirst-quenching water when I need it; there is a bed when I am tired; there is a companion for every man and woman somewhere in the world. In fact, there isn't a passion or appetite of the body that God hasn't an answer for somewhere; be it sleep, or food, or companionship, or love—it's yours for the asking. But the strongest of all desires is to live forever, prosper and be happy. I have never known a man who is satisfied with his task down here. The golden-throated, silver-tongued Italian tenor, Caruso, never sang a song that satisfied him; Paderewski never played the piano in a way that measured up to his ideal. Michael Angelo never chiseled his best; Raphael, Dore and the other master painters never were satisfied with the colors of this life or the execution of them. I never knew a preacher to preach a sermon or pray a prayer that satisfied him. There is no perfection here; yet we long for it, we strive in vain to attain it. But in that land where the sun never sets and the rainbow never fades all our dreams will come true.

AUCTION OF SOULS

Some men sell themselves high, some low, and some give their souls away. You do not have to die to lose your soul. There are many soulless men and women who walk the streets today, those who, in an effort to gain the world, have lost their souls. Alexander, at the age of 33, had conquered the known world. It shook beneath the tread of his mighty armies until he had planted his banners on the ramparts of every city. But he died, it is said, in a drunken debauch, losing both his soul and the world. Caesar led his Roman legions triumphantly through every country and planted the eagles of Rome over every capitol. He crossed the Rubicon and became Rome's mightiest citizen, but he sold his soul to the mad passions and ambitions of life until when he died at the hands of supposed friends, at the base of Pompey's statue, the great poet said of him: "Now lies he there, with none so poor to do him reverence." Napoleon defeated the Germans, twisted the British lion's tail, crossed the Alps with his brilliant soldiers, imprisoned a pope, jerked kings from their thrones and filled their palaces with his brothers and kindred; he drenched Europe in blood and tears, set up governments and knocked them down as men playing ten pins, but he sacrificed the wife of his bosom to promote his mad ambitions and died a lonely prisoner on Saint Helena. I might call the names of Hannibal, Byron, Edgar Allen Poe, Shakespeare and many others who, for a while, seemed to gain the whole world and lost it, with their souls.

The story of the Tapestry Weavers on the other side of the sea beautifully illustrates man's work on earth and his reward in heaven:

IMMORTALITY

Let us take to our hearts a lesson,
No lesson can braver be,
Than the ways of the tapestry weavers
On the other side of the sea.

Above their head the pattern hangs,
They study it with care;
While their fingers deftly work
Their eyes are fastened there.

They tell this curious thing besides
Of the patient, plodding weaver.
He works on the wrong side evermore,
But works for the right side ever.

It is only when the weaving stops,
And the web is loosed and turned,
That he sees his handiwork
That his marvelous skill is learned.

Ah, the sight of its delicate beauty,
How it pays him for all of his cost;
No rarer, daintier work than his
Was ever done by frost.

Then the master bringeth him golden lire,
He giveth his praise as well;
How happy the heart of the weaver is,
No tongue but his own can tell.

The years of man are the looms of God,
Let down from the place of the sun,
Wherein we are always working
'Till the mystic web is done.

Weaving blindly, but weaving surely,
Each for himself his fate;
We may not see how the right side looks—
We can only weave and wait.

But looking above for the pattern,
No weaver need have fear,
Only let him look clear into heaven.
The perfect pattern is there.

And if he will keep the face of the Savior,
Forever and always in sight,
His toil shall be sweeter than honey,
His weaving is sure to be right

PUT GOD FIRST

When at last the task is ended,
And the web is loosed and strewn.
He shall hear the voice of the Master.
It shall say unto him "Well done."

And the white-winged angels of heaven,
To bear him thence shall come down.
And God for his wages shall give him
Not coin, but a golden crown.*

---

*Selected.

CHAPTER V.

THE HOLY SPIRIT

But they rebelled and vexed his holy Spirit: therefore he was turned to be their enemy, and he fought against them. (Isaiah 63:10)

When the yellow fever was scourging our fair land, thereby menacing its health and happiness, our good doctors came nobly to the rescue, and showed us the way out of our distress. They have ever stood guard over our land, until today typhoid fever, diptheria, scarlet fever, smallpox and, in fact, most infectious diseases have been conquered, and long years have been added to human life. It is simply miraculous to contemplate the feats of modern surgery that today bless the world. In whichever direction we may turn we find that the world's needs have always been met by some man or men who are willing to "count not their lives dear" and to answer the cry for help. The world's commerce demanded greater power. There was Fulton and steam; shorter distances, and there was Bell and the telephone. Marconi and the wireless; the world was groping in darkness and the answer was Edison and the electric light. And when it looked as if coal and petroleum would soon be exhausted, the answer was Madame Curie and radium. So for every need there is help near by.

IT WAS NECESSARY THAT HE COME

But we find with our enlarged liberty and freedom enlarged perils, and today there is a restlessness abroad, a contagion of sin, which if not properly and quickly treated, threatens our entire existence. With the spread of knowledge, the march of science and the coming of luxuries, of ease and modern conveniences, the world is forgetting God —leaving Him out of its plans—until there are serious signs of a breakdown of the moral dykes. Even our statesmen and statisticians and our Napoleons of finance, are saying, "Back to God; we need spiritual leadership. Where is Moses?" They recognize the impotence of earthly power, be it monetary, political, social, academic or scientific. While dare devils may fly five miles a minute through the blue sky; while scientists may weigh the ponderosity of swinging, singing planets, discover the secrets of atoms, electrons and protons, yea, they may give us Big Berthas, lethal gas and much enginry of destruction; yet they all confess that, while they may discover life and in turn annihilate it, possibly, may reorganize the world's limitless resources, they cannot give life, neither do they operate in the realm of the soul—that part of man that will live after the stars are cold.

We live in, and thank God for, a really progressive world. New knowledge means mastery of the world of all nature. We know more of philosophy than did Aristotle, or Plato, or Seneca; we know more of mathematics than Euclid; more engineer-

THE HOLY SPIRIT

ing than Archimedes; we know more astronomy than Copernicus, or Galileo. This progress has taught us vast self-reliance. We do not need God now, many are saying. But progress without God will ruin the world, has well-nigh done it already. Look at Germany. For pure and lofty character we must still go back to Christ. Your new knowledge can not make Pauls or the first martyrs; your new knowledge can tell you facts, but cannot interpret them. What has science to say about origins? Can it supply motives or inspirations? What can it say about death and destiny? There is but one interpreter of these things—Jesus Christ.

Jesus' vicarious sacrifice was not only a most tragic and spectacular scene in which he played the leading part, but was the most unselfish service He rendered during His sojourn on earth. Every member of the human family is forever indebted to Jesus, the regal strategist. Napoleon, Julius Caesar, Alexander the Great led men to die for the cause they advocated, but Jesus showed them how to die, and at once showed his faith in the consummation of the plan of God. Christ reconciled the breach between an offended Father and His rebellious children; He finished His work, both practical and passive and turned over to human hands the work of bringing the world to God. This important task, this tremendous responsibility, was quite beyond the capacity of mere man, acting and working in the role of human beings alone. Jesus knew this and promised them the Holy Spirit, who would prove a very present help in every hour of need. The Holy Spirit was to take the place of Jesus; in fact, the word herein translated Comforter is a strong one, and carries with it a very rich and full meaning. Comforter means "one called alongside of," or "called to another," one who constantly stands by one's side as a helper, counsellor, sympathizer and friend.

THE HOLY SPIRIT'S ARRIVAL

Let us return for a moment to Pentecost. Jesus was crucified and buried, but he had also risen from the dead and companied with the loved and trusted disciples in a tentative way for forty days, bade them a very tender and affectionate good-bye and was caught up in the clouds. It would be difficult to conceive of a more lonely and cheerless situation than that which confronted the disciples. The original twelve in number had been restored; they together with others numbering one hundred and twenty, were groping in the gloaming of some deep mystery. They had been told to await the coming of the Holy Spirit, or power from on high. They had no adequate idea of what it all meant; they were just waiting in their loneliness, for Jesus told them to wait. An attitude of expectancy with unceasing prayer was theirs, no doubt coupled with fear. At the end of ten days, or on the fiftieth day, meaning Pentecost, the Third Person in the Trinity came officially among men, and he will remain among men until Jesus shall appear. His coming at Pentecost was in the fullness of power.

THE HOLY SPIRIT

These simple minded fishermen from the humbler walks of life, filled with fear, hunted like beasts of the forest, were no longer cowering; they became as bold as lions, no longer hiding in upper rooms and out-of-way places; no longer fearing a hated and corrupt priesthood, but boldly charging them with the death of God's dear son. Here was a coterie of men so completely changed as to be new creatures indeed. The exhibition of this new power was due to the coming of the Holy Ghost upon them, and out they swept, filled, thrilled, empowered; raising the dead, healing the sick, casting out devils and in Jesus' name forgiving sins.

HE IS A PERSON—HE IS OMNIPRESENT

The Holy Spirit is the greatest ruling force or dynamic among men today; if only men are willing to company with him. The attributes of will, mind, love, care, concern, render the Holy Spirit a personage. Nothing is more common than for us moderns to deplore the fact that we were not fortunate enough to live in the former times when God dwelt in holy Sinai, or pavilioned in the clouds, or framed in the smoky mountain; these, we think, were the days. Oh, we say, if we could only have lived when Jesus trod the earth and ministered to men! But those days, after all, were not the best. They were glorious, it is true, but we have privileges now that were not among the things revealed in the long gone primitive days. God, it is true, was near by, in prophet and priest, type and shadow; Jesus was in Palestine, and his mission of mercy was the finest and fittest of all time; but much of his most noticeable work was local in character. But today the man who is lost goes down in spite of the fact that God has appealed by the mouth of every prophet and by the teachings of every priest; yea, Jesus Christ has exhausted every means that could be contrived by the hierarchy of heaven. Then as a climax of even divine effort, after the most momentous sacrificial offering which can be contemplated by any mind, human or divine, he sent the Holy Spirit to woo, to win, to strive, to convict, convert, regenerate, empower, comfort. The triune God is seeking man. The richest provision which could possibly be made for the children of God has come to full fruition with the entrance of the Holy Spirit upon his office.

TODAY THE BARS ARE ALL DOWN

It has been the privilege of a favored few in all ages to court privileges among the petty monarchs of the earth. By these trifles they have thought themselves honored. Others have enjoyed the loving favor of Jehovah and have prophesied in His name, while others minister at His altars at stated times and convenient season. These likewise have been greatly honored as co-workers with God, the founder and builder of the universe and the common Father of us all. But these honored servants were few in number in the olden times. The great masses of mankind enjoyed no such distinction and had no such opportunities for service. But today the bars are all down, every child of Adam may sit

THE HOLY SPIRIT

down with Deity if he will. God is in the earth in the person of the Holy Spirit, and offers counsel and companionship to all. Heaven has come down to men. Don't stand looking forward to a time on the other side of death—to enjoy the divine presence and inspiration—while the Holy Spirit stands hard by and we may have the full fellowship of the divine every hour we live if we only open our hearts. The Wesleys did, and we see the dynamic which saved the world. Jonathan Edwards, Charles G. Finney and the gentle Moody are examples of God's amazing grace in action.

HE IS THE DYNAMIC OF GOD

In the oil fields I have seen men "shoot the wells." They place a capsule of dynamite or nitroglycerine in the "dry hole," and cautiously let it down, and when they are ready they touch it off. It seems from the explosion and expulsion that the very bowels of nature are being hurled into the air. But that dynamite has cracked the earth on all sides for quite a radius and opened every possible outlet for the golden juice to flow. I have seen God's dynamite planted in a sinner's heart and when fired, out comes obscenity, dishonesty and in fact all kinds of errors. And then there flows from his heart streams of living water. His heart is clean and his spirit is right. I have seen, so have you, this power, this dynamite, dropped into the heart of a great city and Sunday shows and baseball parks are closed, golf links deserted and churches are filled with eager seekers after truth.

I was conducting a series of meetings in Pine Bluff, Arkansas, some years ago. The people were nervous and uneasy over the encroachment of the Arkansas river. It looked as if a good part of the best business section would go into the river. Day by day and week by week the menace became more acute; something had to be done and that quickly. After a conference, secretly held, it was agreed that the river bed must be changed if Pine Bluff was to be saved. Several of the most prominent men of the city agreed to undertake the dangerous task of turning the stream to another channel. A few men quietly left town one night and went away up the river from the city and planted sticks of dynamite, enough to accomplish the feat. When touched off the reverberation sounded like the judgment was on, but with a mighty rush and roar the river changed its bed and Pine Bluff was saved.

There is a stream, a river of worldliness, that is eating its way into the home and church life of our people and constitutes one of the many modern menaces which the church must deal with. Dancing and card playing and Sabbath desecration are working havoc with our young people. Oh, for this river to be turned from its menacing course to the proper channel of usefulness! Who will plant the T. N. T.? Who will fire it? There is a stream, a river of doubt and skepticism, that is eating its way with insidious stealth into our schools and colleges and universities. Where is the dynamite to change its course? Who will fire it? There is a stream, a river of materialism, that is sweeping on in majestic power, bearing away upon its swollen bosom millions of men and women. Where, oh where, is the dynamite to change its course? Who will fire it? If an aroused nation is the church's opportunity, then this is our day.

HIS SYMBOLS

Notice a few of the symbols of the Holy Spirit: Water, revivifying, thirst-quenching, cleansing, germinating water. Does not the church need this? Wind, which sometimes comes in silken zephyrs, again in howling hurricanes. Thus He often comes. Lydia, that seller of purple, had her heart opened with gentleness, while an earthquake shook the jail and released Paul and Silas. Oil, which dedicates, sanctifies, sets apart, lubricates, heals. Does not the church need this? Fire, that illumines, consumes, transforms, energizes. Oh, for our sins to be consumed, our lives transformed, energized and illumined by the Holy Spirit! The dove, too, is used as a symbol. The dove is the cleanest of all birds; has no weapons of offense or defense, a great home-builder; rapid in flight, monogamous in life and sweet of song. The dove stands for peace, and so does the Holy Spirit stand for the Prince of Peace and begs a sin-cursed world to accept the Dove of Peace, the Son of God. Rain and dew. Fertilizing abundant rain; imperceptible, noiseless, permeating dew. A voice, pleading, warning, guiding, crying.

OUR ATTITUDE TOWARD HIM

We know his attitude toward us. Through Him every preacher hears the call to preach the gospel or go to the mission field. Through Him every song that moves the heart is given. Through Him we have comfort, consolation, when sorrow enters our home. Through Him sinners are saved and the church built up. He is waiting today, longing to enter and bless us. But our attitude toward Him is the saddest page in the world's history. Men turned first from God when under His government; then they repudiated God's dear son, foully murdering him. But today men are doing to the Holy Spirit what the men of other days did to God and to His Son. We can lie to Him. Ananias and Sapphira did. We can quench Him; many have. We can vex Him, as my text indicates, and we can blaspheme against Him, which sin is never to be forgiven in this world nor the world to come.

HE WILL BE A WITNESS FOR OR AGAINST US AT THE JUDGMENT

Not only does He draw, convict, regenerate, guide and teach us, He baptizes also, and we are told that at the last day He will be a *Witness* either for or against us. Jesus Christ will leave the mediatorial throne and occupy the judgment seat, and the Holy Spirit will stand hard by, and as our names are called He will witness for us, if we believed on Jesus Christ; against us if we neglected, rejected or scorned the mercies of God.

THE HOLY SPIRIT

Spirit divine, attend our prayer,
  And make our hearts thy home;
Descend with all thy gracious power;
  Come Holy Spirit, come!

Come as the light: to us reveal
  Our sinfulness and woe;
And lead us in those paths of life
  Where all the righteous go.

Come as the fire and purge our hearts,
  Like sacrificial flame;
Let our whole soul an offering be
  To our Redeemer's name.

Come as the wind with rushing sound,
  With pentecostal grace;
And make the great salvation known
  Wide as the human race.

Come as the dove, and spread thy wings,
  The wings of peaceful love;
And let thy church on earth become
  Blest as thy church above.

CHAPTER VI.

SAMSON

But the Philistines took him, and put out his eyes, and brought him down to Gaza, and bound him with fetters of brass; and he did grind in the prison house. (Judges 16:21).

Although the children of Israel had again done evil in the sight of the Lord and had been delivered into bondage for forty years, God once more pitied them and determined to rid them of Philistine oppression. Hence that visit of the angel to the wife of Manoah, announcing the coming of Samson, whose eventful birth would be the beginning of deliverance. Oh, how thrilling, is the strange record of this mighty man! I do not think it would hurt humanity to ponder that great lesson on dietetics given Samson's mother before his birth. I am sure posterity would be better off. For in the miraculous generation of this great physical giant, even God had respect to certain physiological laws.

Samson was the strongest man that ever lived. You might take every pugilist and gladiator and champion wrestler of the world and pit them against Samson, and they would fall before him, helpless as babes. How we read in wonder and admiration of the way he resists the treacherous attempts of his enemies to take his life, and puts them to flight; how he so uniquely burns their cornfields; how, with the jawbone of an ass he slays a thousand men, and how, at midnight, he bears away on his broad shoulders the very doors and posts of the city gates! But we are sorely shocked as we read how this giant suddenly becomes an imbecile in the hands of a little weak woman. He who could put to route an army of men, lifts the "white flag" and falls powerless before the flattery of one woman. But in this, Samson is a type of all mankind. Each person on earth has a weak place in his character somewhere. And right there the devil will unlimber every gun of hell. Paul recognizes this fact and exhorts us to "lay aside every weight and the sin which doth so easily beset us." The negro preacher was not far wrong when he said, "the sin which doth so easily upset us." We all have our "upsetting" sins. There are many men to whom Delilah would not have been a temptation. Their weakness is strong drink. There are others over whom liquor usurps no dominion, but who will fall before the passion of gambling. Then again, I have met men who would die rather than gamble, drink or be impure, yet they declare it impossible to keep from swearing. Yes, every man and woman has at least one weak spot which should be very strongly fortified.

Samson's weakness was very apparent. And I think for treachery and deceitfulness Delilah "wears the bell." I think she would enter smart society, were she living, judging her life and the lives of the so-called society women of today. Hear me! Though she had warmed him in her snowy bosom; though her beautiful arms had been clasped lovingly around his neck; though her ruby lips had thrilled him again and again—yet she had a heart as black as hell! Just listen to the recital of this tale of treachery and lies as recorded by the sacred historian, and you will agree with me.

And it came to pass afterward, that he loved a woman in the valley of Sorek, whose name was Delilah.

And the lords of the Philistines came up unto her, and said unto her, Entice him, and see wherein his great strength lies, and by what means we may prevail against him, that we may bind him to afflict him; and we will give thee, every one of us, eleven hundred pieces of silver.

And Delilah said to Samson, Tell me, I pray thee, wherein thy great strength lieth, and wherewith thou mightest be bound, to inflict thee.

Samson said unto her, If they will bind me with seven green withes that were never dried, then I shall be weak, and shall be as other men.

The lords of the Philistines brought up to her seven green withes which had not been dried, and she bound him with them.

Now there were men lying in wait, abiding with her in the chamber. And she said unto him, The Philistines be upon thee, Samson, And he broke the withes, as a thread of tow is broken when it toucheth fire. So his strength was not known.

And Delilah said unto Samson, Behold, thou hast mocked me, and told me lies; now tell me, I pray thee, wherewith thou mightest be bound.

And he said unto her, If they bind me fast with new ropes that never were occupied, then I shall be weak, and be as another man.

Delilah therefore took new ropes, and bound him therewith, and said unto him, The Philistines be upon thee, Samson. And there were liers in wait abiding in the chamber. And he brake them from off his arm like a thread.

And Delilah said unto Samson, Hitherto thou hast mocked me, and told me lies; tell me wherewith thou mightest be bound. And he said if thou weavest the seven locks of my head with a web.

And she fastened it with the pin, and said unto him, The Philistines be upon thee, Samson. And he awakened out of his sleep, and went away with the beam, and with the web.

And she said unto him, How canst thou say, I love thee, when thine heart is not with me? thou hast mocked me these three times, and thou hast not told me wherein thy great strength lieth.

SAMSON

"And it came to pass, when she pressed him daily with her words, and urged him, so that his soul was vexed unto death;

That he told her all his heart, and said unto her, There hath not come a razor upon my head; for I have been a Nazarite unto God from my mother's womb; if I be shaven, then my strength will go from me, and I shall become weak, and be like any other man.

And when Delilah saw that he had told her all his heart, she went and called for the lords of the Philistines, saying, Come up at once, for he hath showed me all his heart. Then the lords of the Philistines came up unto her, and brought money in their hand.

And she made him sleep upon her knees; and she called for a man, and she caused him to shave off the seven locks of his head; and she began to afflict him and his strength went from him.

And she said, The Philistines be upon thee, Samson. And he awoke out of his sleep, and said, I will go out as at other times before, and shake myself. And he wist not that the Lord was departed from him.

Oh, the mighty power of woman for either good or evil! Few indeed are those men who can stand before the flattery and bewitchery of a beautiful and cunning woman. Oh, the reckoning awaiting woman at the bar of God, for her influence over man! I am glad to place beside this "lewd woman of the baser sort" the gentle, modest Ruths and Esthers of the bible and of life, who exemplify woman's power for good.

THE BLINDING NATURE OF SIN

"But the Philistines took him and put out his eyes." Sin is inexplicable. It is appalling, it is puzzling. Why will a man prefer his lips blistered with oaths rather than have them hallowed by prayer? Why will a man drink, gamble or, upon the altar of lust, sacrifice that which he so much appreciates in his mother—purity? Can you explain why a pure, sweet, innocent girl will permit some black-hearted, lecherous scoundrel to put his arms around her in the ball room, when probably the skunk had them around some "scarlet woman" the night before? I dare you to explain it. Some one please tell me why a woman will give cards respectability by her presence and magic touch when she knows that social card-playing leads often to black-leg gambling? Why will any man or woman sin against God? I believe it can be explained in one way only—they have been blinded by the "god of this world."

There are two beings who are ever striving for the supremacy of man's heart. One is moved by love and pity, the other by revenge and envy—God and his arch enemy, the devil. Paul a long time ago asked a question which was to the point: "Oh, foolish Galatians, who hath bewitched you?" He called it "bewitching them." It means the same thing, who hath blinded you? Surely the old world is under the mesmeric spell of Satan today, judging men and women by their daily conduct. Yes, there are two mighty competitors for man's heart and life. Let me give you a test by which you may prove whether it is God or Satan appealing: The devil offers immediate reward; God never does. Not that there is no reward for righteousness in this life, for there is; for "Godliness is profitable unto all things, having the promise of the life that now is, and that which is to come." But the great reward, the final reward, that glorious reward, reserved for the faithful of all ages, is to be awarded on the last day. Now, the devil is a great old devil and is mighty smart, but he is too cunning to offer you something hereafter. He knows every one will know he is a liar, if he offers anything beyond this present life, for he will be too busy receiving his own just reward of eternal damnation to look after you or any one else. Hence his appeal is altogether earthly and present. I am free to admit it is strong. He is forced to make it so. His only chance is immediate reward. Like the pottage Esau ate, it was for the present only. There can be no pleasure in yonder's world, remembering your sins here. What good will your dancing do you in eternity? Do you expect to derive dividends from your impure life here, after you are dead? Why, men, you shudder now when you think of some of the dark deeds you have committed! They haunt you tonight! How much would you give to be able to blot from memory's record your past sinful life? And the longer you live the more you will abhor it. The pleasures of sin are but for a season. Sin is sweet in your mouth but bitter in your memory. Now, look at the other side a moment. There is comfort in recalling the good acts of your life. How they cheer you along its dusky way! Did you ever drop a nickel into the cup of the blind beggar who sat by the way? How that little act gladdens your heart tonight! But remember the ultimate rewards for such is to be given yonder. Yes, we are really rewarded for righteousness twice —here and hereafter. My girl, you know you would not be willing to have placed in your obituary, "She was the best dancer and card player in town." You flinch! Why? Because you know all such things belong only to this world. The devil blinds the young woman with the glitter and glamour of social life, and whispers to her, "Enjoy yourself now while you are young and pretty." She is thrilled with the idea of present reward and happiness! Of course he very artfully keeps from her the awful result of such a course hereafter. She is blinded! Into the cesspool of worldliness she plunges, ofttimes never to rise again!

Take this young man just budding into strong manhood. The devil tells him that it is degrading to work, and that the goal is so far away. "Just gamble, and then you will have fine clothes now, money now, diamonds now, success now." It looks reasonable. He is caught, blinded, poor fellow! At last he goes down in awful disgrace and ruin and irremediable woe and anguish! But, men and women, what are the foolish pleasures of this world compared with the eternal joys of heaven?

>   Go wing your flight from star to star,
>   From world to luminous world,
>   As far as the universe spreads its wall;
>   Take all the pleasures of all the spheres,
>   And multiply each through endless years:
>   One minute of heaven is worth them all!

But the devil blinds them to the grand glories of heaven, by appealing to their lower natures with present reward. And it does seem to a poor, blinded sinner that present pleasures excel present self-denial. He fails to see through to the greater reward for righteousness, for the devil has impaired his vision. Talk to the average sinner about meeting his God, and you will see that he has been completely blinded by some infernal power, and that he can appreciate only the present. I once heard of a wicked woman who was addicted to strong drink. She had two sweet little girls, one of whom was blind. She would send them out daily to beg money in order that she might buy rum. One evening when they had returned from their street begging, the mother asked how much they had got. Little Helen, the blind one, said, "Here is mine, mama, please don't scold me." "How much have you got, Pearl?" demanded the mother of the other daughter. "Oh, mama," cried the trembling child, who was only used to oaths and blows, "please don't beat me; I have not got as much as sister, for she is blind, and when she says, 'Please help the little blind girl,' why, they just put a heap of money in her cup." "Yes, you little huzzy," cried the brutish mother, "I'll make you blind, and then you can get the money." Pearl, seeming to know what was coming, ran under the bed, but this mother caught her child by the feet, pulled her out and, with a hat pin, put out her beautiful little brown eyes. And amid the terrific, heartrending screams of the poor, unfortunate girl, the mother hurled her away, saying, "Now you can beg, you little devil." But do you know that the devil is blinding men and women just as effectually as did this insane woman her child? Oh, the blinding power of sin! If I could get you to see yourself as we see you, as you really are, and as God sees you, I believe you would be saved!

I once read the story of a beautiful, sweet girl of only sixteen singing summers, whose tresses were golden and whose eyes were honest and blue. She loved a noble boy; his name was Jack. One beautiful moon-bathed evening, while aeolian music gently filled the spacious church building, she leaned proudly upon his arm and walked to where the minister was standing, who pronounced them man and wife. Congratulations were many, and the couple was happy. They moved to a distant city. One night Jack came home with his breath tainted with wine. Lillian wept and begged him not to touch it again. He gently kissed his girl wife aside, declaring that he would never make a drunkard. The same old story—he made a drunkard. From their beautiful, palatial home on the principal street in the city, down, down, down, till they lived in a little hovel on the bank of the river. Money all gone, friends all gone, but she loved him still. One rainy Christmas morning she was standing at the window, wondering what she must do. Cold, hungry, deserted she thought of mother and of her girlhood home. The tears were falling fast. Staggering, stumbling along, she saw Jack coming. "Oh, merciful God," she cried, "is that the boy who was once so noble and brave? Oh, Jack, I love you, darling; why do you drink?" She hastily opened the door and he fell in a drunken stupor at her feet. She looked at him lying there in his filth and vomit, and contrasted him now with his once imperial bearing. "Oh," she cried, "if he could only see himself now he would never drink again." With a woman's intuition and love, she ran quickly to a photographer's and said, "Come with me, sir." When he arrived and learned what she wanted, he said, "Madam, you don't want his picture taken as he is now, do you?" "Oh, sir," she said, "that's just what I do want. I want him to see himself as he is." When the picture was finished and given to the woman, she burst into tears of joy and exclaimed, "This will work the cure." She placed the picture on the mantle and awaited results. The next morning he was sober, but sick. He was about to start out for the day when his eyes fell on the picture. He looked at it for a minute. It seemed to dawn on him who it was. "Lillian, Lillian," he cried, "who is this?" Lillian knew her time had come. She said. "Jack, who does it look like?" "It looks like me. Where did you get it? Who took it? Lillian, is that really a picture of me?" She threw her arms around his neck and cried out, "Oh, my darling Jack, it's all that is left of you. I had it taken so that you could see yourself as you really are." Pressing his happy girl-wife to his bosom, he kissed her lips, as in days of yore, and said, "Lillian, if I look like that, by the grace of Almighty God, not another drop of that damnable stuff shall ever go down my throat." He saw himself as he really was!

A certain society, in order to gain admission for a missionary to some African tribe, sent some trinkets to be bartered with the natives. Among them was a pack of those little hand mirrors that ladies use. The natives had never seen their faces before, except in the waters of some lake or stream. The news of this wonderful instrument was spread abroad until the missionary was invited by tribe after tribe to visit them with this wonderful glass. It happened that, away in the interior, there was a princess who had been told that she was the most beautiful creature the sun ever shone upon. So when she heard of the missionary and his glass, she sent for him that she might see her beautiful face. But the truth was she was a most hideous creature! When he arrived she took the glass and went into her hut to take a good, long, rapturous view of her charming face. But when she looked into the glass and saw the truth concerning herself, with her royal fist she dashed the glass to pieces, and then banished the missionary, and made a law prohibiting looking-glasses to enter the domain. Some people just don't want to know the truth about themselves. That's the reason some men hate to read the bible. It tells the truth about them, and condemns their wickedness. I know that some of you men would be scared nearly out of your senses if you could see yourself as you really are. I heard of a man who thought that the judgment day had come, because he saw the stars falling, or rather he thought they were falling. He called to his wife to get up and get the bible right quick. She made the mistake of getting a black-back mirror instead of the bible, which had a black back. When the poor, pallid, stricken sinner saw his white face and blood-shot eyes in the mirror, he screamed, "Wife, the devil has come, the devil has come!" Oh, if you could only see yourself as you really are it would wake you up.

Mr. Moody tells the story of his little son who wanted to go to Lincoln park with him. "Papa," said the little fellow, "if you will let me go I will let mama wash me." Now, you know he was anxious to go, was he not? "All right, son, go and let mama wash you, and when I come back from town I will take you." The little fellow had his bath and went out on the front porch to wait for his papa. Boy like, he got tired of waiting and, seeing the pump in the yard, he went to it and drew some water and began making mud pies. Of course his hands got dirty and he didn't want to wipe them on the front part of his dress where he could see it, so he wiped them behind. Thus he played and played till he heard the buggy coming and, running to the gate, exclaimed, "Papa, I am ready to go." Mr. Moody, seeing his dirty face and soiled dress, said, "My son, you are as black as a pot; I can't take you." "Oh, no, papa," said his son, glancing at the front part of his dress, "I am not dirty. Mama just now washed me." Mr. Moody declared it impossible to convince him till he took him into the house and stood him up in front of a great big mirror and said, "Now, don't you see you are too black to go?"

So it is with men and women. They think because they present a pleasing front before the world that their life is all right. How anxious we are to appear clean before men, but how little we care how we appear before God! Oh, sinner, stand in front of God's looking glass and see yourself as you are and then, like blind Bartimæus of old, you will cry, "Thou Son of David, have mercy on me."

A sad story is told of the Rev. W. H. Milburn, the blind and eloquent preacher, so many years the popular and much beloved chaplain of congress. He went to London to consult some eminent oculists and to ascertain if it were possible for him ever to see. They could offer no hope. However, one of them suggested that he attend the great meeting of oculists from all over the world, to be held in Paris the next week. Mr. Milburn went, and there he met a world-renowned oculist from Germany. Mr. Milburn knew that if anyone could help him this famous specialist could. He told Mr. Milburn to come to his office in Germany and there he would discuss the matter with him. He went. There he was told he must be put on a certain diet for six months and he prepared for the first operation. Nothing daunted, Mr. Milburn remained right there for the six months on a special diet. At the end of this time the first operation was performed. "Now," said the specialist, "you must be placed on treatment and diet for one year longer, at the end of which time I will again operate, and you then will be able to see, I am sure. You may go back to

America if you like; just follow the directions, and come back in one year and I will operate." The preacher was happy in expectation. He followed closely the orders and looked longingly to the day when he would be made happy as he was freed from his blindness. Imagine the shock when told one morning before sailing for Germany that the famous oculist had just died! With his death had died all hope of ever seeing in this world. Only one man capable of healing him, and for that opportunity to slip was indeed genuine sorrow and bitter disappointment. But, poor blind sinner, there is only one Being who can give you your sight. Don't let the opportunity pass. Jesus can help you. He is anxious to help you. Will you let him? While he will never die, you will, and with your death dieth all hope.

> Tomorrow's sun may never rise
> To bless thy long-deluded sight;
> This is the time, oh then be wise,
> Be saved, be saved tonight.

I read somewhere this beautiful story: A little boy named Charley, who had been born blind, said to his papa one evening, "Papa, is the oculist coming to examine me tomorrow?" "Yes, my boy; I went to see him, and he is to come and examine you in the morning." The next morning the specialist, whose fame had preceded him to America, arrived at the home of little Charley, the only child of rich parents. When the examination was over, Charley said, "Doctor, do you think I shall be able to see?" The oculist said to the father, "I would not inspire hope where there is none, but I don't see why your son may not see. Don't give him any supper or breakfast tomorrow, and in the morning at 10 I will come out and perform the operation." It was not hard to get Charley to abstain from eating, so charmed was he by the hope of seeing. He was in his snowy bed when the surgeon and his assistant arrived. When the anaesthetic was applied Charley said, "Take it away, it tastes so bad." He was told he must inhale it that he might not feel the pain. "Well, mama, you and papa hold my hand and I will take it," said the little fellow. So on either side of the bed stood the fond mother and father, each holding a little trusting hand. When he had become thoroughly narcotized the doctor bade the parents leave the room. Then, dipping his knife into the antiseptic, he lifted the lid and began cutting away that foreign, filmy substance which had prevented sight. He then quickly placed thirty-two bandages over his eyes. Opening the door he beckoned the anxious parents and said, "It is over; remove one bandage each day, and when you remove the last one your child will be able to see as well as you or I." When Charley awoke he said, "Oh, mama, it's dark as ever; I can't see." They explained the situation to him. How long the days were! When all the bandages had been taken off but ten he said, "Mama, I am going to tear these off and see your sweet face right now." "Oh no, my son," said she, "the light would be too strong and might reblind you." Finally the last day dawned. The oculist came to see the result of his work. "Madam," he said, "let the first thing he sees be something beautiful; it will make a lasting impression on him." They took him out into the flower garden where the air was filled with intoxicating fragrance from the prodigal flowers, and where the sun was pouring down a golden sea of loveliness. The mother, gowned in a beautiful morning dress, stood in front of him, while the father stood near by. As the doctor clipped the bandage and it fell to the ground, Charley looked around a moment, and then cried out, "Oh, mama, is this heaven, is this heaven?" "No, my darling son, this is your home." "Oh, mama," said he, "why didn't you tell me it was half so beautiful?" "We did try to tell you, my boy, but you were blind and could not see it." Ah me! We talk of the gold-paved streets of heaven, her jasper walls and gates of pearl; the songs of the holy angels and the pure white throne of God, and you say, "I don't understand you; what do you mean?" Oh, sinner, you are blind, and in the dark! Come to Christ, the great eye opener, the great oculist of heaven, and receive your sight, and join that innumerable host which today sings so triumphantly:

> At the cross, at the cross, where I first saw the light,
> And the burden of my heart rolled away,
> It was there by faith I received my sight,
> And now I am happy all the day.

THE BINDING NATURE OF SIN

Not only did they blind Samson, but they bound him. How much like sin! I am preaching to men and women here tonight who are bound in every faculty of their mind and attribute of their soul. Oh, the binding power of sin! How we Americans love to sing:

>My country, 'tis of thee,
>Sweet land of liberty,
>Of thee I sing.

And yet we scarcely find a man who is not bound by some vicious habit. America is a land of slavery rather than of freedom. We have cigarette fiends, morphine fiends, cocaine fiends, coca-cola fiends, whisky fiends, patent medicine fiends and fiends too numerous to mention. There are boys who have been bossed by their passions till they look like idiots! Manhood all gone! Bound, bound, bound!

I was preaching in the state of Florida when I asked a little boy about ten years old to come to the platform. He did so. I asked him to sit down in a chair near me. As he sat down I grabbed him and, almost before he knew it, I had him tied hard and fast to the chair. I told him to get up. Of course he couldn't; I told the audience that was the way the devil had done two-thirds of the people in the state of Florida. Then to emphasize the utter helplessness of a person once in the devil's power, I pulled the boy's hair and twisted his nose and finally turned the chair over with the boy in it. Of course the lad thought I had gone mad. He was thoroughly scared. I then turned to the crowd of boys on the front bench and said, "Shall I let him go or hold him?" "Hold him, hold him," cried the boys. I said, "That's what the devil and his infernal gang say about every sinner in this town—'hold him, hold him, hold him!' And what about it, girls?" About fifty sweet little girls shouted out, "Let him go, please." "Yes," I said, "that is what God and the good people always say, 'Let him go, please.' But, I said, "No, I will not let you go. I don't care whose boy you are, I will not let you go." About that time we had a sensation sure enough. A little woman came running toward the platform with an open knife, quickly cut every rope that held him, and then kissed him and said, "Now you are free." She then faced the audience and said, "I have a boy somewhere in this cold world today who is bound with sin. Oh that some one would cut the cords that hold him and let him come home to me."

A crowd of young people were out walking one afternoon when one of the young men saw a huge rattlesnake lying in one corner of the fence. He slipped up and quickly seized the monster by the neck, and holding him tightly, waved him toward the party of young people, saying, "You had better run; I am going to put him on you." "Throw him down, George, he will bite you," cried a young girl. "Oh, I am a man," said George. "I could squeeze his head off. Look at me." He then began shaking the reptile till it was in a furious rage. You could see his black, dancing eyes, his quivering, forked tongue. His body was wriggling for freedom. While George's hold was steadily weakening, the snake slowly but surely was crawling through his hand.

George saw what was coming, but alas! too late! He called for help, but the snake had already thrown his tail around George's arm and, turning his vicious head, plunged his venomous fangs into the boy's body—and he was dead! What a true picture of sin! I have seen the young men of today take the pack of cards and play with them. "Oh, I will never make a gambler," they say, but, alas, they do! I have seen them take the sparkling cup and sip it. Mother has said, "My boy, that serpent will bite you." "Oh, mother, I will never make a drunkard." But I have seen them buried in a drunkard's grave, and tonight they are in a drunkard's hell! I have seen the young girl toy with the dance and declare it would never hurt her, and I have seen her mother bowed down in sorrow and disgrace. Oh, the old serpent of hell, how he binds our precious boys and girls with fetters of galling brass!

What is liberty? Men make it mean to do as you please. Never was there a greater mistake. Liberty has its foundation in morals. The man who is living as he ought to live is a co-ruler with God Himself. A man has no right to do wrong. There is a law of health. A man has no right to eat just anything he pleases. He must first learn what is best for him—what agrees with him and what does not; he must eat by the law. Civil law is on the same principle. I must regard others or I shall be taken to prison. I have no right to live as I please. Hear me! There is no real freedom except in Jesus

Christ! Science proposes to emancipate the physical man. She has worked wonders. Today we have steam and electricity and machinery in a thousand forms doing the work that once fell to man. They now have only to guide these mighty forces and, like invisible but untiring slaves, they do the world's drudgery. Education proposes mental emancipation. It has accomplished the marvelous. Not many years ago an educated man was rare, now ignorance is a crime. We are an educated people. Look at our universities and colleges and public school systems; at our great libraries and our thousands of daily newspapers all disseminating knowledge. But when science and education and all kindred forces have done their best for man's liberation, they have but reached the prison door of the royal captive, and must wait till "One comes from Edom, with dyed garments from Bozrah, mighty to save." "But if the Son shall make you free, then are ye free indeed!" The love of freedom is in every man's breast. God made you to be a free man, and you cannot be happy unless free. But sin is degrading and enslaving. Come to Christ and He will break the fetters which bind you, and then you can go home to mother, or wife, a free man indeed. Be a slave of sin no longer.

A poor man who had just been liberated from the penitentiary, after serving his sentence, met a boy with a cage of birds for sale. He bought them, and opening the cage door he let each little bird fly away. The astonished boy said, "Sir, what made you pay for them and then turn them loose?" "My boy," he said, "if you had been in jail as long as I have, and had suffered what I have, you would not ask me why I let the little birds go." Sinner, Jesus looks lovingly, longingly, tenderly toward you tonight in your prison of sin. Only let him and he will open the door to everlasting joy, where you can sing:

> Now, I am from bondage freed,
> Every bond is riven;
> Jesus makes me free indeed,
> Just as free as heaven.
> 'Tis a glorious liberty,
> Oh, the wondrous story,
> I was bound but now I am free,
> Glory, glory, glory!

THE GRINDING NATURE OF SIN

"And he did grind in the prison house."

Sin is not only blinding and binding, but it is grinding. Did you ever see on old-time cane mill? It has a long lever to which a mule is attached, and around and around he goes in a circle all day. So Samson, harnessed in fetters of brass and blinded, is grinding at the mill for his and God's enemies. A man stands near by with a whip in his hand to lay a stinging blow on his bare back and shoulders if he dares stop. How humiliating to the fallen hero! Yes, there is a picture of fallen greatness! Made to honor God and to deliver Israel, he betrayed his high trust and is now doing menial service. What a shame! But he is reaping what he sowed. Around and around he goes all day; nearly dead at night he falls down and tries to sleep. I wonder if he dreams of Delilah! Up again at daybreak and grind, grind, grind! Why will a man serve the devil? "The wages of sin is death." When you have given your best service and are worn out he then mercilessly turns upon you, when you are powerless to resist, and grinds you. He not only grinds you, but he causes you to grind your loved ones. Some of you devil-blinded, bound, ground men have been grinding the blood from your wife's heart until tonight she looks like a ghost! What a happy release death would be to her poor soul! Grinding, grinding, grinding! Oh, the mill, of sin is grinding all the time. Young man, you have nearly killed your darling mother! Look at the gray hairs, the furrowed cheeks and bowed form. Mother has not laughed in years. What are you doing? Grinding her to pieces! Listen, boys, the mill of sin is grinding all the time. What is the product? Tears and heartstrings and groans! Great God, help us to stop this infernal mill of sin. And when your body has been ground to pieces, the devil will then take your panic-stricken soul and, with demoniacal laugh, he will drop it into hell where there is weeping and wailing and gnashing of teeth!

One beautiful Sabbath morning, during the world's fair in St. Louis, a man walked into the barber shop to be shaved. Just as his face was lathered and ready for the razor, the church bells began to chime, calling the people to the house of

God. The man leaped wildly from the chair and, rushing out at the door, shouted, "Stop those bells, stop those bells, stop those bells; they shall not ring!" A policeman caught him and said, "What do you mean; what's the matter?" Oh, sir," said the frightened man, "twenty years ago in Old Vermont I killed my father. We quarreled on a Saturday night, and on Sunday morning when he started up to ring the church bell I followed him and away up in the belfry I stabbed him and left him dead. And every Sunday morning for twenty years the church bells accuse me. Oh, stop them, sir, they shall not ring!" Ground by sin for twenty long years! Ah, the grinding power of sin!

But I would not be true to the commission of an all-pursuing gospel if I did not tell you that God heard the prayer of this old warrior, this blind and bound and ground reprobate of sin in his prison house, and enabled him to catch up the broken threads of his former strength and weave them into a muscle with which he overthrew that great building packed with sports, so that it was said he slew more in his death than in his life.

To the aged, the vile or the despairing of my audience, please let me say that such are the paradoxes of grace; such are the stretches of God's mercy; such is His yearning pity toward poor, fallen man, that if you will but call on Him He will abundantly pardon your many transgressions, so that you can leave this world right with God and all mankind.

CHAPTER VII.

THE PRODIGAL SON

And not many days after the younger son gathered all together, and took his journey into a far country, and there wasted his substance with riotous living. (Luke 15:13).

Jesus was the mightiest preacher that ever lived. He knew exactly how to reach the hearts of men and women. I wish I did! I know if I could have sat near him and heard the intonations of his voice, seen the gesticulations of his hand, witnessed the love beaming forth in his eyes as he preached, I could have been a better preacher.

On one occasion when a great crowd was thronging around him, he said: "A certain man had two sons." Right then and there he had the attention of every man and woman before him. Why? Because he had thrown before them the most beautiful of all pictures—a human home.

Some one has said that mother, home and heaven are the sweetest words in the human vocabulary. I have never met a man or woman who did not love home to some extent. You are now thinking of the home of your childhood. Perhaps it was down in the sunny south, where the mocking birds sang and the magnolias bloomed; or it may have been in some southern clime. Somewhere, I do not know where, you do, though, and to you it is home. Your home may not have had the finest of furnishings, your table may not have been always full to overflowing, but it was home, and you love its memory. "Be it ever so humble, there's no place like home." I think of the home of my childhood. It was there the ego of life dawned upon me; it was there I owned my first pony, dog and gun; it was there I started to school; it was there I learned to say:

> Now I lay me down to sleep,
> I pray thee, Lord, my soul to keep;
> If I should die before I wake,
> I pray thee, Lord, my soul to take.

It was there my character was formed, my destiny prepared. I am glad I was reared in a Christian home, where family prayers were heard twice a day. Those golden days, how I love their memory!

We had several rules which I think would be good to practice in all homes. First, we had to be down to prayers each morning, or miss our breakfast. We were always there. Second, we had to get up as early on Sunday morning as on week days. Third, we were compelled to attend church and to sit with our mother. Fourth, we were not allowed to go outside the yard without permission. Fifth, we were not permitted to spend the night away from home. I remember on one occasion some of my boy friends said to me, "Burke, what makes you sit with your mother in the church? Why don't you sit back here with us boys?" I told them I preferred to sit with my mother. They teased me and said I had to do it, that I was tied to my mother's apron strings. So I said, "Well, next Sunday I will show you that

I can sit back here with you." I said nothing to my mother about it. The next Sunday morning as we reached the church door my mother was holding me by the hand. The boys were looking to see if I would keep my word, and, just as my mother started in, I tried to pull away from her, but she only gripped me the tighter and, holding closely to my hand, she began to drag me up the church aisle, to the astonishment of the people and to my confusion and embarrassment. On she carried me, I bucking like a Texas pony. My mother, however, was the stronger, and finally succeeded in getting me to the front bench, our usual place, and sat me down with a bump. My face was burning; I knew the boys were laughing; I dared not look around. My mother, however, seemed to have forgotten the incident and listened to the preacher. After reaching home, she took me into the study and there she proceeded to impress me in several ways, and when she got through "impressing me" I was thoroughly converted, and the next Sunday morning when we entered the church door I didn't wait for her to drag me, but entered in front of her and took my accustomed seat on the front bench.

You think you had the best home on earth, the sweetest mother and the dearest father and the kindest sisters and brothers. I know I did. Why? It was home. Every little ant loves its home, the bee loves its hive, the faithful dog will protect his home with his life. There is a home instinct planted within us. God is the author of the home, and from it grew the government and the church. Settle the home question right, and all other questions will be settled. The first home was in Eden; the last one will be in heaven.

HOME WITHOUT MOTHER OR SISTER

I once read the story of an angel who winged his flight from the palaces above in search of the most beautiful thing that ever lived on this earth. One day he thought he had found it; it was a bouquet of flowers. and with them he soared toward the bars of gold and the throne of God. But when he reached the City Triumphant he found the flowers had withered. Said he, "I was mistaken; surely this is not what I gathered."

Again he came and searched for many years; and one day he thought he surely had found it—a sweet, golden-haired, blue-eyed baby. As he lay upon his mother's bosom he smiled the sweet, childish smile of innocence. "Oh," cried the angel, "I have found it at last! It is the smile of childhood!" And with this he again winged his flight toward the throne of God. But when he had reached there the smile had changed to a cry of pain. Then said the angel, "I will go one other time." And with the beauty and noiselessness of light he alighted once more upon the earth and searched here and there; one day he found it; it was in a sick room; a mother held in her arms a darling little girl, who was dying of scarlet fever. The doctor had said, "Madam, do not catch the child's breath; if you do, you will inhale the disease and will perish also." Just then the little thing turned to its mother and said, "Mama, I am dying; kiss me good-bye." The mother remembered the words of the doctor and looked at her darling as it breathed its last and, with the mother-love bubbling from her heart, she pressed her lips against those of her child, and soon she, too, had died. "Oh," cried the angel, "I have found it, I have found it! A mother's love, a mother's love!" And he winged his flight toward the home of God, and there the mother's love was just as true and pure and holy as when he plucked it from the sick room.

The boy of our text was unfortunate in this respect. I do not see how he stayed at home as long as he did. To my mind, a home without mother or sister is the last place on earth where one could be happy. Mother heard my evening and morning prayer; mother bathed my face and hands; mother sympathized with me when I was in trouble; mother shared my joys; mother fixed my lunch when going to school; mother whipped me when I was "bad;" mother would take me into the room and pray with me. Mother did everything! I do not know how he stayed at home as long as he did, I say, without a mother.

I was passing through Macon, Georgia, on one occasion and went out to see our old home. The house was vacant. As I drew near, loneliness crept over me. The moon was shining sadly down; I walked up to where a window was open and looked in; it was mother's room! I thought of the many times that mother had sat in that room and talked with me, had held me in her arms, had kissed away my tears, and how she had placed her hand on my head and prayed that I might be a good man.

I saw a little boy not long ago down in Mississippi come up and look into the coffin at his mother's dead face and I heard him cry out, "Oh, mother, why did you leave me?" Poor boy! The boy's best friend is his mother. If the boy of my text had had a mother in all probability he would not have left home.

A man was sentenced to hang. The judge asked him if he had anything to say. He arose to his feet, looked around for a moment and he cried out, "Oh, judge, if I had had a mother!" I am glad my mother came along before the flapper type arrived. A woman arose in one of my meetings and said, "Brother Culpepper, I am old-fashioned. I have long hair, my appendix and I wear a petticoat." I wonder if women of today are as good as women of yesterday.

The princess said to Moses's mother, "Take this child away and nurse it for me, and I will pay thee thy wages." Oh, the wages that a mother receives when she looks at her well-trained boy! And what a joy it must be to a boy to be able to say all through life, "My mother nursed me for God." Nursing is physical, mental, spiritual. The poet expresses the greatness of a mother's influence in the lines that follow:

THE PRODIGAL SON

I have worshipped in churches and chapels:
  I have prayed in the busy street,
I have sought my God, and have found Him,
  Where the waves of His ocean meet.

I have knelt in the silent forest,
  'Neath the shade of some ancient tree,
But the dearest of all my prayers
  Was raised at my mother's knee.

I have listened to God in the temple,
  I have caught his voice in the crowd,
I have heard Him speak when the breakers
  Were booming long and loud.

Where the winds play soft in the tree tops,
  My Father has talked to me,
But I never heard Him more clearly
  Than I did at my mother's knee.

The things in my life that are worthy
  Were born in my mother's breast,
And breathed into mine by the magic
  That the light of her love expressed.

The years that have brought me to manhood
  Have taken her far from me,
But memory keeps me from straying
  Too far from my mother's knee.

God, make me the man of her vision,
  And purge me of selfishness;
God, keep me true to her standards
  And help me to live to bless.

God hallow the holy impress
  Of the days that used to be,
And keep me a pilgrim forever
  To the shrine of my mother's knee.*

HE DIDN'T HAVE A SISTER

I am sorry the boy of my text didn't have a sister. What is so refining and helpful to a boy as a kind, sweet sister? I can nearly always tell when I meet a young man if he has a sister. I think this

---
*Selected.

young man, instead of gambling and drinking and carousing and spending his money on evil passions, would have been more gentle and home loving if he had had a sister to play with.

Miriam watched over Moses as he slept on the Nile as tenderly as a mother could have done. She had the sister spirit. Automobiles and picture shows and bathing beaches are today separating brothers and sisters from each other. They seldom see each other now. The enlarged liberty given to woman has brought enlarged peril; and old-fashioned sisterhood has almost perished. Oh, girl, if you have a brother be gentle and kind to him; you may save him from the fate of the prodigal.

BREAKING UP

Precious as is the name of home, and sweet as are the memories that cluster about it, it is likely any day to be broken up—by death, by marriage, poverty or sin. In some one of these ways our little symbol of heaven—home—is shattered. That sad, grating word, good-bye, is uttered, and home is never again the same.

> Once in the days of long ago,
> Days of my whole life the best,
> When the time for sleep had come
> And the house was hushed to rest,
> It was such a happy thought,
> Used to make my heart so light,
> We were all beneath one roof
> When I barred the door at night.
>
> Let the wind moan as it would,
> Let the rain-drops patter fast,
> They were near me, nestled warm,
> From the midnight and the blast;

THE PRODIGAL SON

Not one lingering out of reach,
Not one banished far aloof—
It's a woman's heaven to have
All she loves beneath one roof.

Now tonight the autumn wind
Through the keyhole whistles shrill;
It must roar amongst the firs
In that graveyard on the hill.
Dying leaves are hurled aloft,
Swaying branches knock the pane,
In the pauses of the wind,
Listen! Oh, the rain, the rain!

Now, when bedtime comes at length
To me, sitting here alone,
And the ticking of the clock
Tells how still the house has grown,
Oh how heavy is the heart
That was once so light of yore;
Now—I seem to bar them out
When at night I bar the door.

But our Father surely needs
All His dear ones near Him still;
Are we not at home with Him,
In the house or on the hill?
So I fill my empty heart
With the thought that far above,
Over them as over me,
Spreads one roof of heavenly love.

So I can go up to bed,
Pass the door where once I heard
Gentle breathing, as I crept
Softly by, without a word;
Though the house is silent now,
Though they wish me no goodnight—
We are still beneath one roof—
When I bar the door at night.*

MARRIAGE

When Isaac and Rebecca married, we are told that Isaac's mother had just died, so had Rebecca's father. A wedding sandwiched between two fun-

---
*Selected.

erals. A wedding is a double first cousin to death. If you doubt it, look at the parents on both sides. They know, however auspicious the day and promising the prospects of making a new home, two are broken up. It is said that when Isaac saw Rebecca, he took her by the hand and led her into his mother's tent. If a boy can't take his bride into his mother's room and show her his mother's chair, his mother's bible, and his mother's closet of prayer, he had better not marry her, and if the bride would blush over such holy things, she is not worthy.

POVERTY

Sometimes a boy or girl has to leave home and go to work to help support the family or educate the smaller ones. I feel like praying heaven's richest benediction upon such an one. You are noble, brave and true. I think it right that a boy should look after **his parents when they** need his help. They helped you when you couldn't help yourself. Now return it. But you must not think because you are away from home they don't miss you. Yes, they do. There is an unturned plate and an empty chair —your home is broken up.

SIN

Sin breaks up a home as much as death, marriage or poverty. Sin is a heart-breaker, a home-wrecker and a grave-digger. Sin is silly, secretive, seductive, sexless. Sin is outlawry. There is no school teaching profanity, drunkenness or dishonesty. To indulge in such things you have to dodge everything from your wet-eyed mother down to the sheriff. Sin is a thing whose product you are ashamed of. If a man constructs a great skyscraper, he points to it with pride. A great engineer like Goethals is thrilled when he sees the mighty hounds of the sea passing through the Panama Canal; a doctor rejoices over the recovery of his patient, or the discovery of some marvelous remedy. In fact, every line of honest endeavor carries a glorious reward. But you never hear a man say, "I gave that man his first drink that led to drunkenness; I robbed that girl of her virtue; I taught that boy to play cards, he is now a gambler." Sin is cowardly, unfair, impudent. It will break a mother's heart, wring the roses from her cheeks, the luster from her eyes and the ruby from her lips. It will whiten her hair, furrow her face—that's sin. It takes only one sin to put a man in hell. You say this is unfair. Is it? One vein will empty the body, one mad dog will panic a block, one fly in the soup will ruin the whole dinner, one drunken boy will adulterate the entire yuletide, one sin drove Adam and Eve from the garden, and one sin will break up your home here, and may cause you to lose heaven hereafter.

But you say, I have never broken up my home with sin and disgrace, like many have. I never spent my life drinking and carousing. I am no prodigal, I never left my home. Wait a moment! When you reached the age of accountability, you looked up into the Heavenly Father's face and said, "Father, give me the portion of goods that falleth to me." He gave you memory, will, judgment and a tender conscience. Have you spent these holy treasures in riotous living? Does your conscience tell you you have always lived right? If not, then you, too, are a prodigal and ought to say, "I will arise and go to my Father." There are sins of omission, commission and submission. The prodigal's sin was that of commission. But there are many today, while they are staying at home, are omitting duty, while some are submitting to things in their lives, their family and friends which are not right.

If you have broken up your home here on earth, go to God in genuine repentance and adjust your life with Him, that you may not rupture eternally your heavenly home. Burns expresses my prayer for every family on earth:

> When soon or late, you reach that coast,
> O'er life's rough ocean driven,
> May you rejoice no wanderer lost,
> Your family in heaven.

CHAPTER VIII.

THE GREAT SALVATION

How shall we escape if we neglect so great salvation. (Hebrews 2:3).

On one occasion in Washington I stood at the base of the monument that was erected to the memory of the Father of his country. The tall column seemed to vibrate with the motion of the earth, and as I thought of the mighty deeds of that great man I said, "This is great; this is great!"

I stood on the banks of the "Father of Waters" and bathed my hands in his silvery spray, and as I thought of the fifteen hundred navigable streams that help to swell his bosom in his noble run from Lake Itasca to the gulf, and of the thousands of farms he waters, again I said, "This is great."

I was in Washington when the gentle McKinley was inaugurated president of the United States, and as he kissed his mother's bible and took the oath of office, while thousands of many colored parasols were lowered and men lifted their hats, again I said, "This is great, great!" But salvation from the curse of sin is the greatest and grandest fact in the universe today, this stupendous and ever-widening system of creation not excepted.

'Twas great to speak a world from naught,
'Twas greater to redeem.

The medical experts tell us that the beating tides

of old ocean are linked with the health and comfort of life of this whole world. The scientists tell us that the tides of old ocean are linked to the moon; the astronomers tell us that the moon is geared to the sun and solar system, and that this in turn is belted to some mightier and stabler center. The christian economist has learned what that center is, namely, Calvary—a center to which is turned the eyes of Jehovah Himself, of every angel, of every fallen being and of this whole groaning creation. Well did the apostle say of Christ, "All things were made by Him, and without Him was not anything made that was made."

SALVATION IS GREAT IN ITS AUTHOR

Its very conception is divine, for in this it is as much above the inventive genius of man as, in its application to his varied wants, it is superior to the concocted schemes of Buddha, Mohammed, Confucius and the rest. Mohammed would offer to the man kneeling at his penitent form a dozen virgin slaves for his heaven—provided he glutted his sword in the blood of his enemies. Christ says, "Love your enemies," and He exalts woman to companionship with man.

Yes, this salvation is great in its author. I see a piece of music upon the piano by which I chance to be standing, and I say to the young lady near me, "Will you please play it for me?" As her deft fingers sweep the keyboard and the music and melody fills the room, I exclaim in my ecstasy, "Who composed that?" She glances to the right

THE GREAT SALVATION 121

hand side of the page and says, "Paderewski." "Oh," I say, "of course it is grand and inspiring. It had a great author." On one occasion Dore, the French artist, was passing from one country to another and had to present his passport before he was allowed to cross. Running his hands hurriedly through his pockets, he found he had left his permit. He tried to persuade the man that it was accidental, and that he really had one at home. In vain did he try to induce the man to let him pass. Said he, "Sir, I have a very important engagement and have not the time to return for that card." The man said, "Who are you, anyway?" "My name is Dore, sir." "The French artist?" queried the astonished man. "I am he," replied Dore. "Wait a minute," said the man as he hurriedly ran into the house and returned, holding a piece of paper in his hand. "If you are Dore," he said "draw that landscape yonder." With a few touches of that trained hand, Dore laid upon that paper the beautiful landscape with its blooming flowers and gurgling streams and its distant snow-covered mountains. "Go ahead," said the man, "no one but Dore could do that." Now look at this old world in its grandeur and beauty. How wonderful! Why, surely "the heavens declare the glory of God, and the firmament showeth His handiwork." Who made it? "In the beginning God created the heavens and the earth." The very God who made the sun, the moon and the stars; who clothes the fields, hilltops and valleys with singing birds and purling streams and scent-laden flowers;

who said on the sixth day of creation, "Let us make man," is the Author of this blessed salvation.

IT IS GREAT IN ITS SACRIFICE

It cost God something to redeem man. I think the grandest expression of love extant is recorded in John 3:16, showing the highest sacrifice on record: "For God so loved the world that He gave His only begotten Son that whosoever believeth in Him should not perish, but have everlasting life." He clothed His Son with humanity that we might understand divinity. Christ suffered the ignominious death of the cross that we might be saved. If the good God had had a thousand sons and had given one, it would have been great; but He had only one, and He was much beloved; yet, to redeem man, poor, fallen man, He gave Him to die. "Oh, for this love let rocks and hills their lasting silence break!" I read the other day of a Japanese mother who had a son who could not go to war, as he was compelled by the law to stay and support her. The mother was so anxious to assist her country that she committed suicide, leaving a note telling her son to go and fight for his country. That was sacrifice for love of country.

Now, go to Bethlehem's manger and see the infant Jesus. Follow Him through babyhood and boyhood, and watch Him as He enters upon His holy, sacrificing mission of redeeming man. Hear Him say, "The foxes have holes, and the birds of the air have nests, but the Son of man hath not where to lay his head." See Him as He daily feeds the hungry, heals the sick and blesses all who come to Him, and yet, at evening when the throngs go to their homes, He climbs the mountain and, while the stars keep sacred watch, He talks to God about fallen man. And one morning they take Him out to Calvary and there nail huge spikes through His tender, quivering hands and feet and pinion Him to the cross. Look at Him as the blood drips from His brow where the cruel thorns are piercing! See them: they are raising that cross to drop it into its rocken socket. Hear them—one, two, three—drop! Did you hear it fall? My, what pain! Stop that man, there! Merciful God! He is piercing His precious side. The sun hides his face and darkness prevails over the earth. Listen! He is talking: "Father, forgive them, they know not what they do." What love, what amazing sacrifice!

Think of it a moment. He had to be born in a manger because there was "no room in the inn." Misunderstood and cruelly criticized while living, beaten and spit upon and abused, He was taken out and crucified. His dead body had to be wrapped in another man's shroud and laid in a borrowed tomb, and with spears and swords they even watched it lest it get away from their blood-stained hands. What sacrifice! Oh, sinner, it cost God something to redeem man. I don't see how one could read the thrilling story of Christ's life, His tragic death, and glorious resurrection, which completed redemption, without feeling God's love for the sinner and His hatred for sin.

IT GIVES US DIVINE RECOGNITION

Let me tell you what I mean in a little illustration: I was once passing through the city of St. Louis, on my way to an engagement in the state of Illinois, when I found I didn't have money enough to get to my destination. I wrote a check, signed my name to it and walked up to a bank and handed it to the cashier and asked him to let me have the money. He took the check, looked at it a moment, then said, "What is your name, sir?" I replied, "My name is Culpepper, as you see on the check." "Why, Mr. Culpepper," said he, "I am not acquainted with you and unless you can bring some friend here who knows you and can indorse you, I can't let you have the money." I said, "Sir, I am a minister, and am only passing through, and I don't suppose I know a person in the city, and then, I haven't the time to hunt them up, if I did, as I must reach my engagement before Sunday. But I assure you the check is not bogus." "It may be all right and it may not," said he, "but I am not at liberty to accomodate you unless I know you." He turned and began writing and left me standing there. I didn't know what to do, but I was compelled to have the money. I picked up a directory and looked through the list of ministers' names until I came to a familiarly sounding one and, taking the car, I rode out to where he lived. I hated to go to him with my trouble, as I knew book agents and tramps frequently imposed upon ministers, and I knew, from experience, he would be suspicious at once, as I had often been when one came to me with a tale of woe.. I rang the bell and an elegantly dressed gentleman came to the door. I knew this was the preacher, and I saw I didn't know him. I said, "Sir, my name is Burke Culpepper, and I am passing through the city and—" "Are you the son of John B. Culpepper?" "Yes, sir," I hastened to reply. (Let me say that I was never as proud to be the son of John B. Culpepper as I was then). I then proceeded to explain my situation. "Why," said he, "I shall be glad to assist John B. Culpepper's son any time; come ahead, we will go now." It happened he took me to the same bank which had refused to honor my check. The cashier recognized me and smiled. When the preacher introduced me to him, he opened the little window and extended his hand. I gave it a hard squeeze, took my money and went on my way rejoicing. I have often thought of the incident. When we stand before the great God at last to be judged for our sins, if Jesus says, "Father, I indorse him," how happy I shall be.

Sinner, remember there is but one name given under heaven whereby you may be saved, and that is the name of Jesus. Oh, get acquainted with Him today and then at last you will have this divine recognition, without which you can never pass through the pearly gates or walk the golden streets. "Surely He hath borne our griefs and carried our sorrows; yet we did esteem Him stricken, smitten of God and afflicted. But He was wounded for our transgressions; he was bruised for our iniquities; the chastisement of our peace was upon Him; and with His stripes we are healed."

IT IS GREAT IN ITS ADAPTABILITY

Christianity is the only religion that suits mankind, all conditions and phases of life, any and everywhere. Take this great, grand country of ours, with its telegraph lines, its telephones, airships, automobiles, its wireless, its radio and hundreds of thousands of miles of railroads; its coal fields, its lead veins and its gold mines; its vast system of creeks that turn thousands of mills, its great rivers that whirl a million cotton spindles; its thousands of cities, drawing into their embrace the best brawn and brain of the world, springing into the air like magic and climbing heavenward like a thing of life. Better still, note our educational system, reaching from the southern cross to rock-ribbed Alaska, and from the Philippine Islands in the west to Puerto Rico on the east—our cavalrymen of supervisors and commissioners in the saddle, charging every redoubt of ignorance and superstition, which yields before their flashing steel as darkness before the rising sun. But, rising above all this in grandeur and sublimity, like Alaskan peaks over the gentle undulating foothills of the west, is the cross of the Son of Mary, the Son of God, beaten into a family altar here, where the widow finds comfort for her bleeding heart and bread for her fatherless children; overarching the portals of business with its golden rule, lifting the common clay of our streets and stones from our quarries into temples of worship, where bell peals to bell, spire gleams to spire, chorus answers to chorus, chanting the Fatherhood of God and the brotherhood of man— bringing special promise to the bereaved and outcast, enabling the tottering octogenarian to sing

> E'en down to old age all my people shall prove
> My sovereign, eternal, unchangeable love—

and literally commanding a convoy of celestial attendants through the swamps of Jordan to the home of God, where the whole world will sing:

> Jesus the name high over all,
> In hell, or earth, or sky;
> Angels and men before it fall,
> And devils fear and fly.

IN THE SWEEP OF ITS PARDON

Not only is it adapted to all mankind and to all conditions of life, but it is great in the sweep of its blessed pardon as it saves the individual, enabling him to sing:

> Amazing grace, how sweet the sound,
> That saves a wretch like me;
> I once was lost, but now I'm found;
> Was blind, but now I see.

It takes the drunkard, the gambler, the liar, the thief, the adulterer, and makes them new creatures in Christ Jesus, causing them to love the things they once hated and to hate the things they once loved. When my father and I were in a West Virginia city, holding a series of meetings, I saw a man converted in a way which will illustrate what I mean. When we reached the city, the pastor said,

"Brethren, one of you will stay at Mr. M———'s home and the other just across the street." We wondered why they separated us, but soon found out. When I was introduced to my hostess she said, "As soon as you have time, I wish to speak a word with you in the drawing room." I said, "I will be down as soon as I can bathe my face and brush the train dust off my clothes." When I came down stairs she said, "Brother Culpepper, you may think it strange that we have separated you and your father, but I have an unsaved husband and two wicked boys, and I felt that if I could entertain one of you in my home my loved ones might be saved." I replied, "I will do all I can to assist you." That night at supper I met her husband and two sons. I saw they were "on to the racket" by the way they acted, but I said nothing, only prayed that I might be led to say something which would at least cause them to be friendly to me. You know before you can have a rabbit pie you must first catch the rabbit. As the husband and sons refused to go to church that night I accompanied my hostess. The boys were nice young men. I felt sorry for them. They were following their father step by step, and I knew it would be an easy matter to reach them, could we but get him. The next morning a thing happened which embarrassed me very much indeed. I overslept, and when I awakened I saw Mr. M——— in my room making a fire, or rather striking a match and lighting the natural gas. I said, "What are you doing, Mr. M———? I can make that fire. You needn't bother about me." "Oh, lie down, Culpepper, I thought you might be feeling bad, and I have brought your breakfast." Before I could say a word or get out of bed, he had a silver tray across my lap, and going to the bath room, brought me a hot towel and said, "Let me know if you need anything else." I was mortified. I knew he thought I was lazy. I saw a peculiar smile on his face as he walked out. The boys asked that day at dinner if I was feeling better. Then, of course, I knew their opinion of me. The next morning I was up early and when I heard Mrs. M—— come down stairs I walked out and said: "Mrs. M——, get breakfast ready as quickly as you can." I told her there was but one thing to do to put myself on an even footing with her husband, and that was to take his breakfast up to him, just as he had brought mine to me. She didn't like the idea at first, but I finally persuaded her to let me have my way. She caught the spirit of the occasion and hurried, lest he get up and thereby thwart our plan. She took the same tray and fixed his breakfast and, giving it to me, told me the room in which I would find him. Going up the stairs and opening his room door quietly lest I wake him, I saw him, lying in bed, fast asleep. Setting the tray on a table near the bed, I took a match out of my pocket and struck it, making it pop along the tiling so as to awaken him. It had the desired effect. He roused up and said, "What's the matter?" "Oh, nothing," I said, "I have just brought your breakfast. Thought maybe you were feeling bad and didn't care to get up." "Get out of here, Culpepper." But before he could get out of bed I had the tray on his lap and a towel with which to bathe his face and hands. He saw he was caught and began to laugh. I said to him as I walked out, "What you sow, you will reap."

That night the major and his two sons were at church and I saw they were deeply convicted. The next night they were there, and after my father had preached his sermon on the "Black Horse of Sin" they remained for the after service. I asked the boys to go forward for prayer, hoping their father would come also. Tom said, "I'll go if papa will." "I will, too," said Ed. I walked back to where their father was standing and said, "Sir, I appreciate the hospitality you have shown me in your lovely home, but I must be faithful to you." I then told him that he knew he was standing in the way of his sons, and that for him to start meant they would. He said. "Tell them to come here." When they reached his side he said, "Boys, I have not led the life I should before you and I am sorry, and if you will follow me to Christ, come ahead." Down the aisle of that fashionable church this rich merchant and his two sons came, and knelt at the altar. In a few minutes Tom jumped up and said, "Mother, I have found Jesus." He turned to his brother, and it was but a little time before he had shown him how to accept the Savior. Mr. M—— continued to kneel there. I

THE GREAT SALVATION

said to him, "Sir, you are rather heavy to be kneeling so long. Suppose you sit there on the bench and let me talk with you." He looked up into my face and said, "Let me alone, I want to kneel here until I can again feel as innocent as I did when I knelt at mother's knee and prayed:

> Now I lay me down to sleep,
> I pray thee, Lord, my soul to keep;
> If I should die before I wake,
> I pray Thee, Lord, my soul to take.' "

I left him kneeling, but not for long, for he soon arose, and if you ever heard a happy man shout, he did. Running to his wife, who looked like an angel had melted a rainbow and poured its colors over her face, he said, "Oh, wife, I will go with you to heaven now." As these three strong men were taken into the church the next Sunday and promised to forsake the world, the flesh and the devil, I said to myself, "Thank God for the sweep of the pardon of the love of the Son of God."

> I was once far away from my Savior,
> And as vile as a sinner could be;
> I wondered if Christ, the Redeemer,
> Could save a poor sinner like me.

Yes, this salvation is great in its rescue and reconciliation, giving to the saved man a new perspective, a new purpose, a new power.

A SALVATION OF PEACE

The world today is seeking peace. Ask that merchant what he is after and he will tell you he is trying to make money enough to rest in his old age and have peace. Ask the lawyer, the physician, the banker, what is their goal, and the answer will come back, "We hope to get peace in the end." Every vocation beckons with outstretched arms to all who pursue her, and whispers, "I will give you peace." There is but one thing in this world that will give peace, and that is this great salvation. Look today at the millionaire whose hair is turning gray as he struggles for just one more dollar. The rich are not always happy. You will find more unhappiness among the rich than you will find dissatisfaction among the poor. It was Vanderbilt who, when dying, said, "Wife, now sing, 'Come ye sinners, poor and needy.'"

Neither will intellectual superiority bring peace. Look at the greatest poet that ever lived. How did he die? In a drunken debauch. I today challenge the world to produce a single man who is responsible who can say that he has peace of heart and mind outside the peaceful religion of Christ. But, thank God, the One who said to this sin-cursed world, groaning 'neath its mighty load, "Come unto me all ye that labor and are heavy laden and I will give you rest," is abundantly able to do so.

A man was told by his physician that he could live but a few hours longer. "Well," said the man, "may I be carried out to my flower garden and see the flowers one more time before I die?" The physician said it would not hasten his death, and he was tenderly carried out by loving hands to his garden. One of his friends, standing near, said, "It's mighty hard to leave your sweet wife and children and lovely home, and your beautiful flowers, isn't it?" The sick man said, "My friend, don't you think for a moment that I wanted to come out here because I was unwilling to leave them. I wanted to cultivate my senses, for, if what the doctor says is true, in a few hours I expect to inhale the fragrance of the Rose of Sharon and the Lily of the Valley." He had the peace of God in his heart and what cared he for dying?

Out west on one occasion I was called to the bedside of a dying woman. I said to her, "Sister, you are dying; how is it with your soul?" She looked at me a moment and then, with a smile on her lips, said, "It's all right, sir. I am not afraid to go." You remember it was Patrick Henry who, when his physician said to him, holding a phial containing a very dangerous drug, "There are nine chances against you, for one in your favor, for if this doesn't save you it will kill you." Patrick Henry said, "Wait a minute." Turning away he breathed a prayer and said, "Doctor, I will take the chance." He took the drug. The physician waited near him to see the result. In a few minutes Patrick Henry noticed the blood curdling under his finger nails and said, "Doctor, is this death?" "Yes," said the physician, "you will die." "Well, then," said the great man, "let me show you how a Christian can die." Nothing but religion can make a man die that way.

A poor boy was shot down on the battle field and knew he could live but a little while. His bunkmate said, "George, can I do anything for you?" "Yes," he said. "Bob, I wish you would look in my grip and get the testament mother gave me the morning I left home." When he had done so the boy said, "Now, read over there in the fourteenth chapter of John, please." So he read, "Let not your heart be troubled; ye believe in God, believe also in me. In my Father's house are many mansions, if it were not so I would have told you. I go to prepare a place for you, and if I go and prepare a place for you I will come again and receive you unto myself, that where I am ye may be also." "That will do," said the dying boy. "Just put that bible under my head and if you see mother, Bob, tell her I went home with Jesus."

> Peace, peace, sweet peace,
> Wonderful gift from above,
> O, wonderful, wonderful peace,
> Sweet peace, the gift of God's love.

PUTS A BOTTOM IN THE GRAVE

What would the sad, heart-broken mother do when she kisses her dead baby good-bye, if she didn't expect to meet it again? We have all lost loved ones. Our hearts have bled as we followed our departed dead to the silent, sleeping city, and laid them beneath "the tongueless silence of the dreamless dust." But as we walked away something whispered, "You will see them again where there will be no more sin, sorrow or separation.

Voltaire, Renan, Gibbon, and many others would have us believe when we bury our loved ones we shall never see them again, but Jesus, who is the resurrection and the life, would have us sing as we are leaving this sin-blighted world:

> On the happy golden shore,
> Where the faithful part no more,
> When the storms of life are o'er,
> Meet me there;
> Where the night dissolves away
> Into pure and perfect day,
> I am going home to stay,
> Meet me there.

What would the poor widow, who has struggled all alone, trying to rear her children righteously, do, if there were no family reunions beyond the grave? "Earth hath no sorrow that heaven cannot cure," since Christ put a bottom in the grave. Oh, thank God we shall meet our loved and lost some sweet day!

NEGLECT

If all I have said is true, how shall you escape if you neglect so great salvation? Neglect is the biggest thief on earth. You expect to be a Christian sometime, but not now. Neglect, neglect! The condemnation against the five foolish virgins was not one of wickedness, but they just neglected to have oil in their lamps. If the farmer neglects to sow his seed in the spring-time and avail himself of the gentle showers and warm sunshine, he cannot escape want and distress later on. If the lawyer neglects to look after his work, soon will be heard no more the clients' footsteps crossing his threshold seeking his advice. If the youth neglects to study and apply himself diligently while his mind is fresh and susceptible, he will come to manhood's estate poorly prepared to grapple with life's conflicts.

> Of all sad words of tongue or pen,
> The saddest are these, It might have been.

I once heard the story of a drunken man who caused the death of hundreds of men, women and children in a very peculiar way. An opera house was packed with eager listeners, who were suddenly thrown into a panic by the cry of "Fire!" The vast audience arose and started to leave the building, when this drunken man shouted, "That's part of the play; you needn't leave." Thinking they had acted hastily, they sat down, laughing at their supposed fright. In a few seconds, however, one of the performers ran to the platform and shouted, "Get out; you will be killed!" A second time the audience rose and started to leave, when this man again said, "Oh, that's part of the play; I have seen it before." They sat down, but in a little while the building collapsed, killing many innocent people. Sinner, don't think it a part of the play as I preach to you tonight, for, hear me, you cannot escape if you neglect so great salvation.

Upon a drawbridge in one of the northern states this sad incident occurred. The bridge keeper received a telegram, telling him to keep the bridge closed, as a special train was due soon. A friend came up in a yacht, and said, "Hello, Henry, let me through." "I can't," replied the man. "I am looking for a special in a few minutes." "Oh, it won't take me long to run through, and you haven't heard it blow yet; let me through." The keeper said, "All right, make haste." And drawing the bridge, his friend passed through. But my! He saw that train coming round a bend and, before he could possibly get the bridge back and locked, it swept down and plunged into the river many feet below. As the bridge-keeper from above saw strangling men, women and children, and knew his neglect of duty was the cause, his brain reeled and in a second he was crazy. Pressing his head with his hands, he walked up and down, looking at his helpless victims below and repeated over and over, "My God, I wish I hadn't!" Sinner, if you neglect this great salvation which is able to save you, and at last break into hell, you will walk the burning marl of damnation and cry out in bitterest wails, "Oh, God, I wish I hadn't! I wish I hadn't!" No longer neglect this proffered salvation, but give your heart to God tonight. Listen, sinner, listen:

> In the silent midnight watches
> List thy bosom door;
> How it knocketh, knocketh, knocketh,
> Knocketh evermore.
>
> Say not 'tis thy pulse is beating;
> 'Tis thy load of sin—
> Jesus 'tis that knocks and crieth,
> "Rise and let me in."
>
> Death comes on with reckless footstep
> To the hall and hut;
> Think you death will tarry knocking
> If the door is shut?
>
> Jesus, waiteth, waiteth, waiteth,
> But the door is fast;
> Grieved, away thy Savior goeth—
> Death breaks in at last.

> Then, 'tis thine to stand entreating
> Christ to let thee in;
> At the gate of heaven beating,
> Waiting for thy sin.
>
> Nay, alas, thou guilty creature—
> Hast thou then forgot?
> Jesus waited long to know you—
> Now He knows you not.*

And I want you to remember that you don't have to be a big sinner to be lost. The text doesn't read, how shall you escape if you swear, or drink, or gamble, or steal, or lie, but it reads, "How shall you escape if you neglect so great salvation?" Turn to God tonight, I beg you before it is too late.

ESCAPE

Escape what? Escape the sinner's life. Of all lives the most unsatisfactory is the sinner's life. Escape what? Escape the sinner's death. How awful to die without God. A poor sinner lay dying and just before he breathed his last, he cried out, "Oh, wife, can't you help me?" She said, "What do you want, my husband?" "Oh," cried the poor fellow, "I am lost, lost, lost! You can't help me now, I am going to hell." How horrible, I say, is the sinner's death. A young man was working on one of the piers of the bridge which spans the Missouri river at Kansas City, when an accident occurred which cost him his life. Just before he died, he was carried to a little tent nearby and laid on a cot. When told he must die he requested that someone pray for him, but no one seemed to be able to pray. He asked if they would read to him from the bible. They

*Selected.

THE GREAT SALVATION 139

searched about a little and couldn't find one. "Then," said the dying man, "boys, can't you sing me a song about Jesus?" They told him they didn't know any. "Oh me," he said, "must I die away from home, without prayer, a song or a verse of scripture?" But thus he died.

Escape what? Escape the sinner's awful doom. How indescribably terrible to hear God say, "Depart ye cursed, I never knew you." My text declares in the very question it propounds that it will be impossible to escape, if you neglect this great salvation.

CHAPTER IX.

WINDING THE REEL

The evolutionists tell us that the "survival of the fittest" is an inexorable law of nature. The Christian economist, however, will tell you that the rescue of the unfittest is the law of grace. The urge of rescue is almost universal today.

We have seen men and dogs cover themselves with glory as they crossed frozen deserts to carry the salvation of antitoxin to a diphtheria-besieged Alaskan town. Airplanes and dogs raced in rivalry to get there first. The sympathy of a nation was recently mobilized in an attempt to rescue an entombed explorer from a cave in Kentucky. Searching parties in steel motor ships took the air in an effort to find the north pole and bring back the daring, dauntless Amundsen. An earthquake in Japan shakes the gold out of American pockets. The cry of help knows no boundary line of creed or color.

Jesus came to seek and to save the lost. The stories of the lost coin, the lost sheep, and the prodigal son discover to us the amazing depths of mercy that flows from the heart of God's dear Son.

While the romance and results of gospel preaching often escape the printed page and defy human tabulation, in almost every preacher's ministry there has occurred miraculous manifestations of supernatural power which would constitute expert testimony as to the power of God to rescue.

> Rescue the perishing, care for the dying,
> Snatch them in pity from sin and the grave;
> Weep o'er the erring ones, lift up the fallen,
> Tell them of Jesus the mighty to save.
>
> Though they are slighting Him, still He is waiting,
> Waiting the penitent child to receive;
> Plead with them earnestly, plead with them gently;
> He will forgive if they only believe.
>
> Down in the human heart, crushed by the tempter,
> Feelings lie buried that grace can restore;
> Touched by a loving heart, wakened by kindness,
> Chords that are broken will vibrate once more.
>
> Rescue the perishing, duty demands it;
> Strength for thy labor the Lord will provide;
> Back to the narrow way, patiently win them;
> Tell the poor wanderer a Savior has died.

The following incidents have come under my observation during my evangelistic campaigns:

HARRY HOLMES

The most beautiful sight on earth to me is a sinner accepting Jesus Christ. You may have your towering mountains and your daisy-covered valleys, your babbling brooks and deep canyons, from which to gather your inspiration, but give to me an old-fashioned revival, where the altar is filled with penitents seeking God! In the spring of 1916, just before Easter, I was invited to Harrisburg, Arkansas, to conduct a revival. The meeting was held in the Methodist Church, the largest auditorium in town. We were having large crowds both day and night. I was literally "shelling the woods," for there were some conditions that needed heroic treatment, and I felt led of God to preach along lines that are sometimes not very popular. Much had been said about ballot box stuffing, bootlegging and other forms of vice, and the situation was getting serious. The churches were paralyzed by worldliness. There were cliques in the little town, and no one seemed to think it was his or her business to raise a warning voice.

One morning, accompanied by my assistant and director of music, Mr. John U. Robinson, I walked into a department store to make a purchase. A salesman came to wait on me and, after I had made the purchase, he told a very obnoxious story. I shall never know why he felt called upon to tell such a story in our presence. As I walked away Mr. Robinson said to the man, "Did you know that was Brother Culpepper, the evangelist?" The salesman, who was the proprietor of the store, no doubt felt ashamed of having been so thoughtless, but made no effort to apologize.

The day services were being held in the forenoon, and that very morning this man who had told the story, closed his place of business and he and his entire force were out to the services. I did not refer to the unpleasant incident. That night he was back again. He came for several days and listened as I preached on Jesus, the sinner's friend. He seemed to catch every word that I uttered and watched my every move.

On Good Friday afternoon I was in my room reading when there was a knock on my door. Upon

WINDING THE REEL 143

opening the door I found a young man, who asked me to take a ride with him—out to his father's farm in the edge of town. I did not know the young man, but as the sun was shining and the air balmy I thought it would be a good time to fill my lungs with fresh air.

Some miles out we came to a farm house and, standing at the gate, was the merchant who had told the story and with him were sixteen others. I did not know what I was getting up against, but the only thing to do was to go ahead and take care of myself as best I could. Getting out of the car I was met by one of the men who said, "I am glad you came; follow me." We went to a nearby cottage, where I was introduced to the tenant and his wife. I then had the strangest of feelings to steal over me. Harry Holmes, for it was he who told the story and who was now in charge, invited the entire crowd out to the barn. When my father would take me to the barn it was for serious offenses, and I did not relish going to the barn with this strange bunch of men, but it looked as if I had to do it.

Harry Holmes was a former saloon keeper and a very immoral man, but at this time was one of the leading merchants of the town. On reaching the barn the men lined up on either side of the manger. Addressing the crowd, Mr. Holmes said: "Men, it may seem strange to you that I have brought you out here this afternoon, but this is Good Friday and when I was a child mother told me on this day Jesus Christ was crucified. She would read to me the story of the little babe being born in a manger. I have doubted the story until now, but I want to say that this same little boy has been born in my heart today, and I have brought you men, with whom I have gambled and sinned deeply, out here to reverse my life on sin, and I want to know how many of you, my sinning pals, will follow me in this new found faith."

Every man in the crowd rushed up and shook the hand of Harry Holmes and promised him that his God and his Christ should be theirs; that where he led they would follow. He did not ask me to talk, but knelt in the straw and offered the most beautiful prayer I think I have ever heard. A cow with a new-born calf was near and she seemed restless and uneasy at the crowd, whereupon Harry Holmes said: "Old Bess, do not be uneasy; we are not going to hurt you or your calf; I will never kill either of you. I want you to know that there has been born in my heart the Christ that was born in Bethlehem's manger some two thousand years ago." One of Mr. Holmes' boys was there and while his father was talking he ran from the barn, while his eyes overflowed with tears. I went out after him. He said, "Papa is going crazy." I told him he was all right and was just coming to himself. Mr. Holmes said he wanted to give his name for the church, and when I made the call that night he and his friends were the first to come forward, amid the shouts of happy mothers and wives.

Harry Holmes is sticking today. He became

president of the local Y. M. C. A., superintendent of the Baptist Sunday school, a deacon in the church and a leader in all church activities in his town.

A LOST CHILD

"A little girl is lost!" was the startling cry which greeted the ears of hundreds of people in a meeting that I was conducting in Caruthersville, Missouri, in 1924.

The revival was in full swing. The entire town and community was aroused, for some things were taking place that made it quite interesting. I was fighting gambling and bootlegging, and there was plenty of both going on there at the same time. The officers seemed powerless to put a stop to it, and blind tigers were no longer winked at, but were run open and above board in many instances.

So hot was the fight that my life had been threatened, but that did not deter me from doing my duty. I had a detective make a map of the town, showing just where whiskey was being sold. I called the officers in conference and showed to them the map and told them if they wanted to clean up the town I would furnish the information. Raids were put on and there were some arrests. The excitement was at high pitch all through the campaign.

One night I preached to several thousand people in the large tent, located on a lot back of the Methodist Church, which was formerly a graveyard, but on account of being in the city it was no longer used for that purpose. Some of the old tombstones were standing, while many had fallen down, the graves leveled and it was no longer regarded as the sacred "city of the dead." At the close of my sermon I asked that the front benches be cleared so that I could make a proposition for those who would accept Jesus Christ to come forward and occupy them. On the front seats were a large number of children. They got up at once and began to find other seats. One little girl, possibly eight or ten years old, who was sleepy, arose and started back to find a seat elsewhere. Those who saw her thought she was going to sit with her mother. The mother saw the child, but just supposed that she would sit down and wait until the services closed.

We had a great service. Scores gave their hearts to God and their hands for the church of their choice. When the crowd was dismissed a large number remained for a few minutes, shaking hands with the new converts, meeting and speaking to neighbors and strangers. The news was given out that a child was lost. A search was hurriedly instituted about the tent, under the platform, in the church and other places where one would likely be, but no trace of the child could be found.

After some time was spent in searching, in company with my assistants, Mr. Sisserson and Mr. Robinson, I went to the hotel to retire for the night, feeling sure that some one had taken the child home. After discussing the revival and also the lost child with my assistants I retired about twelve o'clock. I had not been in bed long before the fire whistle sounded. It was one of those wild-cat whistles—a siren. It was located near the hotel, and as it would moan and groan, going down to a hoarse bass and then rising to a keen, shrill whistle, it would almost make the hair rise on one's head. The prolonged blowing of the whistle alarmed me, and I thought that possibly the whole town was burning up. I looked out through the window but could see no trace of the fire, but the whistle kept getting louder and louder, it seemed to me, making the most hideous sounds imaginable. Soon the church bells began to ring, and then I knew something awful had taken place. I called to my assistants and we were soon on the streets, to find that the child had not been found. Hundreds of citizens gathered at the tabernacle to learn the sad story that the child had not been found. After a conference with the sheriff and chief of police the town was divided into sections and a committee of citizens were sent into each district, with instructions to ring every door bell and ask if they had seen the lost child.

Towns within a radius of twenty miles were communicated with by telephone and asked to keep a lookout for the child. Rumors were flying thick and fast. One rumor was, that the child was seen in a car with two young men. That fired the crowd almost into a frenzy.

My assistants and myself were assigned to the chief of police. There were some six or eight in this party. The territory assigned us was the river banks. We rang the bell of every door and inquired at every shantyboat, asking if they had seen a lost child. The other searching parties were doing the same. The broken-hearted and distressed mother was at home, keeping watch over her other children. The father was among the searchers.

The hours passed and the search continued until every house had been visited but one. This house was situated on the outskirts of the town, at the intersection of two streets. The searching party on one street made sure the party on the other street would visit this house, thus both parties missed it. When the entire town had been covered the searching parties met at the city hall and it was agreed to resume the search after daylight. The father of the child went to his home to tell the wife and mother that the child had not been found. It was agreed before the crowd separated that should any traces of the child be found that the siren would again be blown.

Just as the first streaks of dawn were seen and the young day stood at the gate of the morning, there was a knock at a door—the very door that the searching parties had passed by—and a little girl stood on the outside. When the occupants of the house went to the door she said, "I want my mama; can you tell me where my mama is?" "My dear child, the whole town has been looking for you. Where have you been?" The news that the child had been found was quickly telephoned in, and again the siren was heard! But this time instead of a moan of sadness it had the glad cry of good news—the lost child had been found!

When the little girl left the front seat at the tent she went to a car and, thinking it was her father's, climbed into the back seat and was soon sleeping. The owner of the car and his wife got in and drove home, never looking on the back seat. When they reached their home the car was put into the garage and they went to bed, but did not fasten the door of the garage. When the little girl awakened she got out of the car and went to the house, and it was there she received the information of how the town had been looking for her. She was soon restored to her parents and the town went back to bed, but the lesson was impressed on them that if the whole town would look for a lost child, how important it was that lost souls be restored to the Master.

THE CHURCH IN THE WILDWOOD

Rupert Hughes' insolent article on "Why I Quit Going to Church," is only one symptom of a damnable malady attacking the church today. The church is the only human institution Jesus ever joined. It was through the organized church He carried on His remedial process of salvation. He recognized her imperfections and limitations, but left her intact and said the gates of hell should not prevail against her. Those modernist ministers who are standing in her pulpits questioning the virgin birth of the Son of God and the inspiration of the holy scriptures, ought to have the decency to step down. Let one of this bunch start a revival and he would not have enough people present to play puss in the corner.

They are one of the reasons the church is being sneered at today by so many.

But for the revivals being held up and down the land by Holy Ghost pastors and evangelists the country would be in bad shape. Holy Ghost revivals are saving sinners, sanctifying believers and adding thousands to the church rolls.

In a Missouri city I was urging the people to put God first, accept Jesus Christ as their Savior and join some church. After the service one night a leading business man called on me at my hotel and asked for an interview.

"I was reared a Roman Catholic and educated in a Catholic college. I had heard many times over the Protestant religion held up to scorn and abuse. In my daily contact with the world I had found quite a few Protestants in whom I had utmost faith, and was at a loss to know why such hatred of them should be in the minds of the Catholic priests who were my instructors. One day I was out walking with the head master of the school, a devout Catholic, and I said, 'Father, are there no good Protestants? Will all of them be lost at last?' He replied, 'Son, I would not say every Protestant will go to hell, but I do say the only church on earth is the Catholic; the rest are illegitimate.' I did not like his attitude.

"In a few years I was through school and out in the business world, meeting all classes and creeds. I said I would go to the Protestant churches and hear their side of the matter and judge for myself which is right. In every Protestant church I happened to go I found the burden of their message was the criminality of the Catholic faith. In disgust, Bro. Culpepper, I turned from both and said there are good and bad Catholics, likewise there are good and bad Protestants. Both Protestants and Catholics are too intolerant. I will join neither. So I quit the Catholic church and, not liking the Protestant, I am not a member of any visible church organization, but I have organized a church of my own, and I would like to tell you about it, sir, and ask you if this church of mine is not adequate." I said "Proceed."

"My church," he said, "is panoplied by the blue sky above, its carpet is the green grass, and the golden stars are its altar candles. The trees are the pipes and reeds of my organ through which the silken zephrys play, and the birds are my singers. Conscience rings the bell which calls me to service, and the rain baptizes me. The golden rule is my creed and justice is my text. I have excluded from my church only two classes—the Jew and the Negro. I don't like them and so don't want them in my church."

I said to this fine, misguided business man, in whose home I had dined and whose family are members of the church, "Sir, where are your hospitals for the amelioration of the sick?" "I haven't any," he said. "Where are your colleges located for the training of the young? Who prints your bibles and religious papers?" "My church has no schools or bibles, or papers," he replied. "Who performs your marriage ceremonies and buries your dead?" I asked him. He failed to answer. "And where did you get your creed—the golden rule?" He sat in silence. "It came from a Jew and yet you have excluded the Jews," I continued, "and this outcast Jew was willing to let the poor negro help Him carry His cross to the top of the hill, and there die for you and for me and for all mankind regardless of sex or color or nationality. My friend, your invisible church in the wildwood is a selfish one."

He said, "Brother Culpepper, you have given me something to think about. I will see you later."

The next night he came down the aisle and kneeled at the altar, surrendered to God and said, "I have disbanded my church and I want to join that church which is Christ's bride and worship with the sons of men."

GOING HEAD

I was conducting a revival near a southern city a few years ago. The meeting was gripping the entire town and community. So large were the crowds there was not a building sufficiently large to take care of them and an "al fresco" tabernacle was provided. One of the citizens of the town lived in a beautiful home with a large lawn and his front porch was used for a pulpit and the choir and seats were provided on the lovely lawn of green grass, making an ideal place.

One night at the conclusion of the service, a handsomely dressed man came to the platform, shook my hand and asked if he might have an audience with me the following day. I told him that I would be glad to talk with him. After he left me several came to me and asked what the man wanted. They said he was very wicked and if I could reach him for God and the church it would mean much to the entire community. He was a man of influence and had a wife and two noble sons who were Christians.

The following morning this gentleman called, and I saw at once that he was in earnest. He said he wanted to tell me a story and that my answer to the story would determine some things in his life.

"Yours is the first minister's hand I have clasped," said he. "My wife and boys are members of the church, but I have never taken an interest in the church. I have been busy making money and possibly doing other things that I should not have done.

"My father was a poor man, and an invalid. My mother died when I was but a mere boy, and I was reared on a small farm. We lived in a cabin, with scarcely the necessities of life. I helped my father with the household duties and also worked on the farm. There were few educational advantages out there, two months in the summer was about all the schooling we had. When the crops were 'laid by' the boys who worked on the farm went to school. I attended school in my rags, for I did not know what it was to have a good suit of clothes. Mother being dead, my father and myself did the house-keeping, such as it was. Often the beds would go unmade and everything connected with the house was out of order.

"I attended the country school, but did not go

with the other boys, or rather on account of my poverty they would not go with me. I often felt lonely, and during the recess would stroll out in the grove, to meditate on my condition. I never ate my lunch with the other boys, for I did not have cake and pie, such as they had, but often just a roasted potato. I never tried to excel in my classes, for to do so would but the more emphasize my poverty and call attention to my patched trousers and uncut hair; but I did want to be somebody and there was a longing in my heart to be a real man.

"There was custom in the school that the one who had perfect lessons for a week and stood at the head of the class, would be given as a reward a piece of blue ribbon. This honor was much sought by the boys and girls. One day, as one of the boys walked up and the teacher pinned the blue ribbon on his coat, something seemed to whisper to me, 'Jack, why don't you try and get the blue ribbon, the other boys are getting it.' From that moment my brain was fired with ambition and I determined that I would stand at the head of the class for a week and get the blue ribbon. I had perfect lessons for the entire week, and to the astonishment of the teacher and the pupils I stood at the head of the class. When I got home Friday afternoon, with my heart all aglow over the success I had achieved during the week, my father said to me, 'Jack, you can't go back to school any more; one of the mules has died, I am sick and that field of corn must be cut and shocked.' I felt my heart sink within me, for I was determined on leaving the little sway-back school house to wear the blue ribbon the next day. I said, 'Daddy, I know you can't help being poor, and I know you could not help the mule dying. Mama is dead and we do not have the things that other people have. I am called old man Millikin's poor boy at school. The boys won't play with me because I am poor and my clothes are ragged. I have been at the head of the class all the week and I want to go back and get the blue ribbon. I will come home and cut and shock the corn by moonlight; I want to show them that a Millikin can wear the blue!' My father said all right, and turned away with tears in his eyes. With a heavy heart but a determination that I would wear the blue, I hurried off to the little sway-back, moss-covered country school house. Soon after I got there the bell rang and school was 'taken up.' After the usual preliminaries the teacher began to hear the lessons. I led my classes, as I had done the preceding days of the week. I received the commendation of my teacher and felt my heart well within me as lesson after lesson was recited and I still stood at the head of the class.

"The last lesson of the day was the old-fashioned spelling match, in which the entire school participated. It was the final test, and if I could outspell the school I would be given the blue ribbon. We used the famous old blue back speller. As we began to spell the pupils began to drop out one by one until there were left only two, a little girl and myself. She had on a pretty red dress and I was in rags. The boys, for the first time, lined up with me and the girls took the side of my adversary. Every time the teacher would give out a word we would look at each other, eager to get a chance at it should the other fail. There was a wide gap between the little girl and me, made so by those between having dropped out. The teacher asked us to move closer to each other, and I noted the little girl deliberately folded her dress close to her person to keep it from touching me, and thus the race was on. After a few minutes the teacher gave out a word to the girl and she——missed! I could have shouted for joy, for I knew how to spell the word, and knew that meant I would wear the blue ribbon. She looked at me as if to say 'You miss it, too;' but in my eagerness to show to the school that I could 'go head' I said to her in my mind, 'I am going to spell you down, red dress or no red dress.' The word was given to me and I spelled it. The teacher then called me to his desk and pinned on me the blue ribbon. It was the happiest moment of my life. I gathered up my books and started home, when the teacher called to me and said, 'Jack, where are you going; school is not out.' I replied to him, 'Yes, teacher, it is out for me. I can't come back any more. I know you boys and girls call me old man Millikin's poor boy; you would not play with me or invite me to your homes, but don't forget I went head; I went head!'

"I walked out of that school house while blinding tears washed my face. A hundred yards away I stopped and shook my fist at the little school house

WINDING THE REEL 157

and said, 'You are for rich men's boys and girls, not for me; but I went head just the same.'

"When I got home I told my father that I had won the blue ribbon. He put his arm around me, and while he did not speak, I knew that he was proud of his boy. After a scanty supper I cut and shocked the corn, finishing the task just before daylight. In my soiled and sweaty clothes I went to bed and in my sleep I dreamed of the little school house, the little girl in red and—I had gone head!

"When I became a man I decided to go head financially, and I now pay taxes on one hundred thousand dollars. I also went head in wickedness. I have been a gambler and a heavy drinker. I want your prayers, sir. Since hearing my story I want to know if you think I can go head religiously."

I grasped him by the hand and said, "God bless you, Jack Millikin, yes you can go head." That night after my sermon I made the call and down the aisle came this man, and as he clasped my hand he said "Tell the people that I have come to go head!"

A few years later I was called to his home on a very sad mission. One of his noble sons had just died and the other was quite sick. He met me and ushered me into the presence of his wife who was prostrated with grief. I shook her hand and gave her what comfort I could, and then offered a prayer for the sick boy. We then went into the room where lay the dead young man. My friend asked those present to leave the room and, going up to the casket, this big-hearted, big-brained man talked to his dead son. He said, "Son, Brother Culpepper is here. Daddy is still standing at the head of the class, and I will never let sin turn me down." Amen!

JIM BERRY

The latter part of March, 1921, I was invited to Corsicana, Texas, by the Methodist pastor, Rev. Cullom Booth. The meeting was held in the Methodist church, and while it was not a union meeting it developed into a co-operative one. From the very first the crowds were large, but it seemed to me that I could not get anywhere with my sermons. I had to fight the world, the flesh and the old "daddy devil." For the first time in my experience as an evangelist I became so discouraged that I felt that I had to quit. On Friday night I told the pastor that I was whipped and would close out on Sunday night; that there was no use in my staying longer. When I made this announcement, the presiding elder, Rev. A. D. Porter, sprang to his feet and begged that I stay on. He told the card-players and dancers just where the harm was in those things, and said they were paralyzing the church. The pastor, Cullom Booth, said it would be the disappointment of his life if the meeting should close at this time. Others in the audience insisted that the meeting continue. I did not want to close the meeting for personal reasons, but if I was not doing any good thought I might as well. It was agreed that the meeting should continue for at least one week longer.

I had back of me in the choir four of the leading society women of this Texas city. They refused to give up their cards, claiming they saw no harm in them. The pastor and his wife sat up all one night praying for this quartet. The next day he told them what he had done and one by one they gave it up and became active workers in the meeting.

There was a man in Corsicana, Jim Berry, who was known far and wide as a gambler and bootlegger. He was a blockade runner and had gambled (according to his own statement) on the Mississippi river from St. Louis to New Orleans. He had sold whisky in Dallas and many other places in Texas. One morning I was preaching in a cafe and this man Berry came along. He stopped for a few minutes to see what was going on, when some friends on the outside literally pushed him through the open door. The crowd was so large he could not get out and had to stay and hear what I said. I did not know him, at that time, but if God ever had a good job pulled off on Texas soil I was the instrument used.

There was something in the sermon that seemed to grip this man, and that night he was in church. When I made the proposition for those who wanted prayer to come forward, Jim Berry, to the surprise of everybody, came. After the service several came to me and told me the story of Jim Berry, and said if he could be converted it would mean more to Corsicana than any other one thing. The next night Berry was back again and when the invitation was given he walked down the aisle and made the full surrender.

I was invited by Mr. Berry to hold a service in

his cafe. I was glad of the invitation and the opportunity. Long before the hour for service the place was packed with people and many were standing on the sidewalk in front. The place had formerly been a saloon; the counter, the mirror and the brass rail were still there. The four women who had refused to give up cards, but later did so, helped in the singing, standing behind the "counter." I preached as best I could, and when I had finished Mr. Berry said he wanted to talk. He begged his former associates and friends in vice and wickedness to forsake their ways and join the church. He asked that the ministers present join hands around him and wall him in with prayer. It was a beautiful sight.

I asked Jim Berry if he would make a talk at the Methodist church that night. He said that he had never spoken in a church, but would try. I made the announcement that "Jim Berry would preach in the Methodist church tonight." The crowd was so large that it was with difficulty I got into the building. I will let the Corsicana Daily Sun tell of that service:

"After an old-fashioned experience meeting, in which men and women praised God, Brother Culpepper arose and said he had asked Jim Berry to speak a few words to the audience. He said that Mr. Berry was not a public speaker and begged for him a quiet audience.

"Jim Berry, as he is lovingly called by everybody far and near, and a man whose word has always been as good as his bond, was brought to know Christ a few nights ago in the revival. His was a genuine case of old-time conversion, as his bright, happy face testified when he made the surrender. So happy is he in his new-found peace that he wants to help somebody else. He offered his cafe to hold a service and his friends filled the building early. At that meeting there was a wonderful manifestation of the Holy Spirit, but last night the meeting surpassed anything ever heard of in the history of the christian religion in Corsicana.

"Jim Berry arose, calm and deliberate in his new-found courage, and said in part: 'Brother Culpepper, brothers and sisters, it is a pleasure for me to tell you I am saved. I see some of my kinsfolk are out to hear me preach. I know they think I'm a fraud, but I tell you, boys, there isn't anything to that other stuff, and I know it. When you get into it you can't get away. Don't be stubborn like I was. I don't want to leave you, boys; I want you to come with me. I thank God I'm saved and want to thank all my friends who are standing by me.'"

A beautiful scene followed the remarks by Mr. Berry. I made the call and asked all who wanted to be saved to come forward. Jim Berry stood by my side and shook hands with the scores who came and kneeled at the altar, among the number his two boys. They grasped the hand of their father and said they wanted his Christ to be their Christ.

The following Sunday morning I went to Shady Grove, a church near Corsicana, to preach at the

Sunday school hour. Jim Berry went with us. It was his old home. As a lad he would cut the harness off the horses while the people worshipped in the church. He left there as a boy of fourteen years and had not been back. Jim Berry was one of the speakers at this service, and many came forward to congratulate him on the noble stand he had taken, while others came to confess Jesus Christ for the first time. At the conclusion of the service I saw Mr. Berry go over to a window that was overlooking the little cemetery, and tears were streaming down his cheeks. I walked over to where he was standing and laid my hand on his shoulder. He said, pointing to the cemetery, "My father and mother sleep out there. Oh, Brother Culpepper, I wish they could have lived to see this day."

Jim Berry's conversion transformed the town and county. By his life and work among men scores were induced to join the different churches. Mr. Berry became a Sunday school teacher, and each Sunday morning he could be seen with his bible under his arm going to teach his class of boys the story of Jesus and His love.

Mr. Berry's fame as a sinner was such that Col. Humphries, a wealthy oil driller and a christian, upon hearing of the conversion of Jim Berry, shut down operations and held a prayer meeting, thanking God that the king of bootleggers had been saved, and oil men in that section would have relief from the ravages of rum.

I invited Mr. Berry to be with me in my meetings at Dallas and Tyler, to tell the story of his conversion. It was so much bigger than many would believe I wanted them to hear it from his own lips. Many wicked men were reached through this wonderful convert.

In the early spring of 1924 I was in my home in Memphis and Judge Tarver, a close personal friend of Mr. Berry, called me over the long distance telephone and told me that Jim Berry was dying. Judge Tarver said, "Jim says tell Brother Culpepper I'm going home; it's all right. I'll meet him up there." Just before the breath left his body Judge Tarver, bending over him, caught these words, "Culpepper, Culpepper." The spirit of Jim Berry winged its flight to that land where the sun never sets and the rainbow never fades, and somehow heaven has been nearer and dearer since I know that Jim is up there waiting to welcome me to the city of God.

BURYING A HATCHET AND HAMMER

Several years ago I was conducting a revival in Forrest City, Arkansas. The town had been split over a murder case years before and was apparently hopelessly divided into two factions and cliques, which had not only paralyzed the churches until they were seemingly dead, but as far as I could ascertain there was not a bank or store or school or home that was not involved in this unholy war of hatred. The town was dead spiritually, socially and financially.

The meetings were being held in the courthouse. After ten days of as hard preaching and praying as

I had ever done, together with the godly pastors, we instituted a season of fasting for the Holy Spirit to come. When He came it was in such power and demonstration we were all amazed. Over five hundred cases of malice were settled.

The men went to the woods and dug up a noble tree and brought it to the courthouse yard and replanted it. Governor McRea and Chief Justice McCullough wired to reserve rooms at the hotel. They wished to see this political, social and religious hatchet buried. By the hundreds they poured into Forrest City to see the miracle. Two little girls, dressed in white, stood near by with hatchet and hammer in hand, while Judge Brooks Norfleet delivered the oration, and at the conclusion of his great address they dropped both hatchet and hammer into the deep hole near the roots of the tree, while many shovels were pushing in the dirt. The people said we will not only bury the hatchet, we will also bury our hammers and stop knocking each other.

The Daily Herald has this to say concerning the revival. I only quote it that men of today may see God's power is still available to those who will pay the price:

"Last night's meeting was the greatest and grandest of the Culpepper series. Old men who have traveled far and wide, and who have attended many meetings, declare they have never known anything like it.

"It is not just the thing, perhaps, to say that it is a Culpepper meeting, because as this good man said

WINDING THE REEL

in the beginning, 'We are going to make this a meeting for God and the salvation of souls,' and as to how well he has kept his word let the host that has acknowledged Christ under his ministry attest.

"This is no ordinary revival where the ladies have all the religion. The ladies have been forced to the rear for once and the men are in the lead, and they are men who know how to lead.

"As a consequence the meeting has passed beyond the faith of the most sanguine of our citizens. Brother Culpepper says it has gone beyond him also.

"This does not mean that the ladies have not been a power in this, the greatest of all great meetings held in Arkansas, but it simply means that many of the best and most influential citizens here are leading in this great spiritual upheaval that has shaken Forrest City and rattled the very teeth of the devil himself.

"The most dramatic scene ever witnessed on or off the stage was enacted in the Culpepper meeting at the St. Francis courthouse here last night.

"Circuit Clerk R. W. Payne came in and stood before the people. The man's cheeks were ashen. Upon his face was the pallor of death. His lips were blue. He was wild-eyed. Ladies and gentlemen looked at this man whom they all knew and loved, but last night his ghostly appearance inspired them with awe and they trembled and hid their faces. One lady said, 'Oh, please take me out of here. I can't stand it.' Another said, 'Oh, my God,

Mr. Payne has lost his mind.' Still another said, 'Did you see that unearthly look in his eye? It makes me shudder now. I shall never forget it.'

"Old men looked on horror-stricken. It was a tense situation. The court room seemed to be bulging out at the sides and running over at the top with the influence of the Holy Spirit. Mind you, now, The Herald is talking about sensible men, intelligent men, great big men who know and do things and who never go into any sort of a proposition with their eyes shut.

"It was men of this character who declared that they never saw anything equal to the conversion of R. W. Payne. It was simply staggering in its intensity. The devil had Payne, and he didn't want to turn him loose!

"Mr. Payne handed in a list of names to the secretary of the men whom he wanted to talk to. He had been thinking about them for several days and said, 'When I do come I want to come clean.' The front seats on the rostrum were cleared and the men to whom Mr. Payne wanted to talk were called. (These men had been saved during the revival, and Mr. Payne, who had known them intimately, wanted to question them. Mr. Payne, although a fine man, had been somewhat skeptical). These are the men he called for: Capt. James Fussell, Judge E. A. Rolfe, Mr. Eugene Williams, Mr. T. A. Buford, Senator F. W. DeRossitt, Judge S. H. Mann, Dr. J. F. McDougal.

"When these gentlemen were seated Mr. Payne

WINDING THE REEL 167

started talking incoherently and at random. At first it seemed that nobody present could make head or tail of what he was trying to say. He might as well have been using some secret code or sign language, so far as those about him were concerned.

"It was thought by some that his reason had been dethroned on account of the tremendous conviction he had been under for the past few days. Finally, and long toward the end of the jumbled and frightful harangue, Mr. Payne spoke out clearly and stated, 'Now, boys, all I want to know is this: are we going out together and ring the bell true and fight under the same flag?'

"Still in a seemingly dazed condition, but with a look of complete resignation on his face, Mr. Payne walked over and sat down by his wife and dropped his face into his hands as if he had been completely crushed.

"Following Mr. Payne's dramatic confession Dr. McDougal broke over the traces. The sheriff was seized with a holy laugh. Then the people thought, well, old 'Mack' is gone, too. He's off—such a pity! The sheriff laughed and cried and shouted and finally he let out a yell: 'God's fooled old Payne one time!'

"Nothing to equal this scene has occurred anywhere. The congregation stood upon their seats and for a time pandemonium broke loose in the meeting. It was like touching a match to tinder. Men flocked to the platform to line themselves up with God's people. Big things were happening.

"These were no puny, idiotic, spineless hirelings who were pulling off this stunt. These were big, strong, brainy men who stand at the head of affairs in Forrest City. It meant something. It meant among other things that we are breathing a purer, sweeter and more wholesome atmosphere in Forrest City. It meant that with the winning of Payne we will bury the hatchet just that much deeper and that we will all march out together, ring the bell true and fight under the same flag."

I have recently conducted another meeting in Forrest City. I found Dr. J. F. McDougal the teacher of the men's bible class, Tom Buford is chairman of the board of Stewards of the Methodist Church; Capt. James Fussell and Hon. R. W. Payne have both gone home to God, having died in the faith. Scores of converts of the former meeting are still there, living true to God. Some of my best workers in the last campaign were converts of the former revival.

Beautiful church edifices have taken the place of the former shacks of worship, and in many and lasting ways Forrest City attests the permanency of the benefits of a genuine Holy Ghost revival.

www.ingramcontent.com/pod-product-compliance
Lightning Source LLC
Chambersburg PA
CBHW031354040426
42444CB00005B/285